The New Learning Commons Where

Learners Win!

Reinventing School Libraries and Computer Labs

David V. Loertscher
Carol Koechlin
Sandi Zwaan

You are invited to discuss this book at:

http://www.schoollearningcommons.pbwiki.com

To do so, ask for an invitation to comment
On the front page of the wiki

Hi Willow Research & Publishing

Content current through Aug. 25, 2008

Hi Willow Research and Publishing
312 South 1000 East
Salt Lake City UT 84102

Distributed by:
LMC Source
P.O. Box 131266
Spring TX 77393
800-873-3043
sales@lmcsource.com

ISBN: 1-933170-40-9; 978-1-933170-40-4

In Appreciation

We express appreciation to the many colleagues and students throughout the years who have helped shape the ideas in this book. Many read drafts of this book and recorded ideas on the accompanying wiki.

The authors spent two major multiple-day writing sessions at the Kawartha Pine Ridge District School Board in Peterborough, Ontario, Canada with Diane Istead and Jeff Brown as our hosts. They linked us to so many wonderful people and ideas and are pushing so many great programs into the 21st century.

Contents

The Learning Commons
An Introduction

The Learning Commons
A Justification

It is illogical to imagine an information age school without a fully functioning library serving as the information centre. Guided Inquiry calls for rethinking the function of the school library and the librarian role in transforming K-12 education to meet the demands of the 21st century.
Carol Kuhlthau

School libraries became commonplace in schools during the 1960s when the United States was worried about competing with the Russians for space travel and when an article in *Redbook* magazine reported that Americans spent more on dog food than on library books. Computer labs in schools developed much later as Apples and PCs became affordable.

The advent of the Internet and of ubiquitous computing devices ranging from iPods to iPhones stimulates a great deal of rethinking about how everyone works, learns, and communicates. Why should we, in the world of academia, try to exist without the technologies that are prominent in the world at large? Certainly, the science fiction writers of yesteryear were on target as we now see our computers becoming extensions of ourselves. At the moment there is a disconnect between the personal use of technologies and most educational practice.

The current duel between two major business models gives us incentive to rethink everything. The Microsoft Model and the Google model, two very different philosophies of doing business, are quite familiar to all of us in various aspects of our consumer behavior. In the following illustration, the underlying principles of the two systems are compared in the context of education.

Microsoft Model

Google Model

Microsoft Model
- Command and Control
- Organization Based
- Behaviorist Teaching
- One Size Fits All
- If We Build It, They Will Come
- Program Specific Skills

Google Model
- On Demand
- Client Based
- Inquiry Teaching
- Differentiated
- If They Build It, They Will Use It
- Lifelong Learning Skills

The music industry is a good example of the clash of the two models. For half a century, major labels dominated the recording industry and controlled what albums were put on the market. In today's market, the customer is saying, "I want what I want, where and when I want it." Many musical groups have bypassed the traditional model and turn directly to the consumer. These groups try to "go viral" by using YouTube giveaways of their music. The "If we build it" company markets packages of software that we are expected to use on their terms. The "If **they** build it" company supplies us with a set of tools and we are allowed to creatively build our own information systems. This is the major difference between "If we build it, they will come," and, "If **they** build it, they will use it." The argument for the "If we build it" model is that structure and organization coupled with a service orientation is really what is needed. The argument against the "If **they** build it" model is that it is fragmented, is messy, lacks uniformity, and transfers control to the novice.

Both the school library and the computer lab have been designed on the "If we build it" model with command and control idea as their structure. Stereotypically, librarians have been viewed as "keepers of the books" and tech directors as dictators of their networks. While our service-oriented library and computer professionals ensure that their systems work efficiently under their direction, there are major leaks in the dam. Classroom teachers, unsatisfied with the limited availability of print, build their own classroom book collections and other teachers begin using Web 2.0 tools that bypass the school's central networks. Students bypass both libraries and computer labs by going directly to the Internet that is always there and that always returns an answer to any query. It may be an inferior answer, but convenience usually wins.

Moving Toward a Client-Side Learning Commons

We argue that moving libraries and computer labs toward the client-side, or "If they build it" model, is inevitable. Our clients, both teachers and students, increasingly demonstrate that they are not only comfortable in an "If **they** build it" model information world, but stop using our services when alternatives are friendlier. It is quite possible to clamp down on the customer to insist that they use our systems, but we are generally accessible only during the school day and because of various scheduling practices, by appointment only. Consumers generally select a new store if the current one doesn't have what they want or need or are not open when they have time to come.

A move to client-side information systems is often stalled because of a great deal of fear and suspicion about users: "If you let them on the Internet, they will instantly stray away from their purpose and possibly encounter predators." Thus, systems are filtered heavily in response not only to those fears, but also because of federal laws and the threat of lawsuits.

We argue that administrative and instructional information systems are quite different. Administrative computing needs to be locked against hackers who might cause all kinds of mischief with schedules, grades, or budgets. Instructional computing, however, is quite another matter, since it is in place to facilitate learning. The trend in Web 2.0 applications is toward very safe collaborative digital areas where groups of learners can thrive. However, these are not necessarily served out from district computer networks. While providing these may cause temporary panic for those who want "control," a re-examination is currently in order.

We posit that both adults and young people need to learn to build their own information spaces and to learn to be responsible for their actions in those spaces. Since our clients are under our influence only part of the day, we need to help them learn and help create rules of behavior both in the real world and in the digital world. It would seem wise to teach them how to cross the digital freeway safely because we cannot always be there to help and guide them across. Users with some degree of computer ability already know how to get around the most stringent of controls. It is a myth that Web 2.0 tools and spaces are automatically dangerous.

The flipside of current practice in education is to consider the users and then figure out how the organization can fill their needs and wants. Consider:
- Available on any device anywhere 24/7/365 vs. available on our computers during the school day

- Acquire the books kids want to read vs. acquire the books adults think the children need to be reading

- Filters on "dimmer switches" that can be adjusted in relation to responsibility vs. tightly controlled one level fits all filters

- Totally moveable furniture for instant re-configuration vs. heavy stationary furniture

- Allowing students to check out as many books as they can be responsible for vs. each student is allowed to check out only two books

- Flexible scheduling vs. fixed timetable

- Just-in-time coaching and mentoring vs. after school assistance

- Focus on knowledge and understanding vs. teach to the test

- Collaborative action-research based teaching vs. isolated classroom teaching

- Learning to learn as we teach content vs. teaching content

Going client-side is a habit of mind. It is a conscious effort to think first of the needs of the customer rather than the needs of the organization. Making the shift is not as complicated as one might think. It need not always require years of planning and astronomical budgets as first anticipated. As planners shift from command and control organization, they will find greater potential for creativity and problem solving. Initial fears and blocks are often overcome easily as success builds.

One of the major changes will be the inclusion of clients in the planning, implementing, and evaluation of the changes made. They have to help us build it so they will use it. If they have a stake in it, they will care and be more responsible.

What is the parent's role? Going client side requires that parents understand clearly what is going on and that they are expected to participate in the new system. Consent forms acknowledge that responsibility is a privilege and everyone is involved, supportive, nurturing, and participating in this extension of educational opportunities. Everyone means school administrators, teacher technologists, teacher librarians, classroom teachers, parents, and, most importantly, the students themselves.

Learners Win!

Soaring dropout rates, bored students, and students who choose not to access the computer or library services of the school, create a digital chasm between the digital habits of students and the traditional nature of schooling. Schools must respond to the clients they serve. It is not just an out-of-touch problem. Opportunities to learn, grow, excel, and compete globally demand that this generation of adults learn to boost the opportunities of the next generation. It is time learners won; and, it is time for us as educators to stop being ignored as irrelevant.

Everyone Wins!

It is time that Googlers accept teacher librarians as information coaches. It is time that learners see tech specialists as enablers rather than permeable brick walls. As we, the adults, rethink and reinvent we trust that the best of the pieces from our former library and computer lab will find a place beside and boost the new whole-school learning atmosphere.

The benefits of the Learning Commons to the entire school community and teaching and learning will be explored in each of the subsequent chapters. It is worth noting before we begin our journey that by creating a Learning Commons space, and culture the hard work of school improvement is more readily attainable. Funding, resourcing, implementing and tracking of programs can radiate from one common space. At any time administration can measure the pulse of improvement in one spot rather than chasing down initiatives all over the school.

It's time to reinvent so that everyone wins.

Over to You. Discuss with us at: http//schoollearningcommons.pbwiki.com

- *In the book: Inside Steve's Brain* by Leander *Kahney published by* Portfolio (Penguin Group), 2008, we get a picture of how Steve Jobs saved Apple. What business model did he use and how could we reinvent using some of his ideas?

- What behaviors are you seeing in learners that encourage us to rethink current practice?

- What do the kids at your school say about the need to reinvent education?

- How is the move toward open-source applications encouraging rethinking?

- What is crowd sourcing? Could it help us rethink? Clue: Read the book: *We Are Smarter Than Me* by Barry Libert, Jon Spector, Don Tapscott, and a bunch of other folks (Wharton School Publishing, 2007).

- What about *The World is Flat?*, or, *Wikinomics*, or, Daniel Pink's *A Whole New Mind*?

Resources

Foundational Ideas
- Foley, Mary Jo. *Microsoft 2.0: How Microsoft Plans to Stay Relevant in the Post-Gates Era*. Wiley, 2008.

- Vise, David and Mark Malseed. *The Google Story: Inside the Hottest Business, Media, and Technology Success of Our Time. Delta, 2006.*

Other Resources
- Friedman, Thomas. *The World Is Flat. 3.0: A Brief History of the Twenty-First Century.* Picador, 2007

- Kuhlthau, Carol, Leslie K. Maniotes, and Ann K. Caspari. *Guided Inquiry: Learning in the 21st Century.* Libraries Unlimited, 2007.

The Learning Commons
A Tour

As one enters the Learning Commons, the first impression differs greatly from that of the traditional library or computer lab. Immediately, we notice a completely flexible learning space where neither computers nor books get in the way. If we were to come back in an hour, we might see a completely different configuration of individuals and groups of youth, adults, or both, busily working, consulting and collaborating. The buzz in the air is both purposeful and casual and it is a mix of learners both adult and student engaged in a wide variety of activities.

Upon further examination, we discover that two major functions are being accommodated simultaneously in the Commons. The first is the Open Commons, and the second is the Experimental Learning Center. Each is controlled by its own calendar of events but coexists in a busy real place while also extending into virtual space. The faculty, in consultation with the learners, creates a powerful learning environment through a combination of innovation, learning tools and learning science. Thus, it is a micro R&D center of testing, experimentation, and exhibition connected to a larger network of educational research and practice.

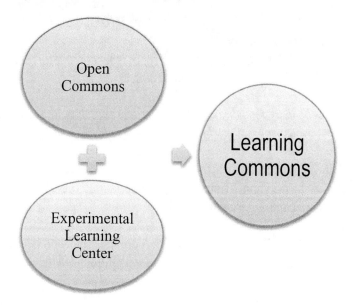

The Open Commons

Constructed around client-based principles, the Open Commons is a service center planned by both the youth and the adults, drawn there by its inviting and collaborative atmosphere. Obviously equipped with wireless access, both students and adults are using personal digital devices as individuals, small groups, or as large groups. Students stream in and out of the Open Commons during the day and are virtual visitors at night as they take advantage of the vast array of information sources, various service centers, production capabilities, and communication possibilities.

In one area, we notice an expert bar staffed by students and adults who are consulting with individuals or small groups needing assistance with software and hardware. In another area is the mentor bar where adults—faculty, staff, and volunteers—are providing individual group guidance on projects, assignments or just personal advice and encouragement. At any given time we notice that beyond the support staff and volunteers, learning specialists are also coaching.

It is easily apparent that the Open Commons is an extension of the various classrooms of the school; a place everyone owns, works, and collaborates in a collegial social environment. The space runs on its own calendar to avoid chaos and overcrowding. Students have been major players in the creation of policies and behavior guidelines that make the environment inviting and conducive to learning. These same policies exist not only in the physical space of the Commons but also into its virtual equivalent. These emphasize a welcome and purposeful enticement rather than a practice of exclusion.

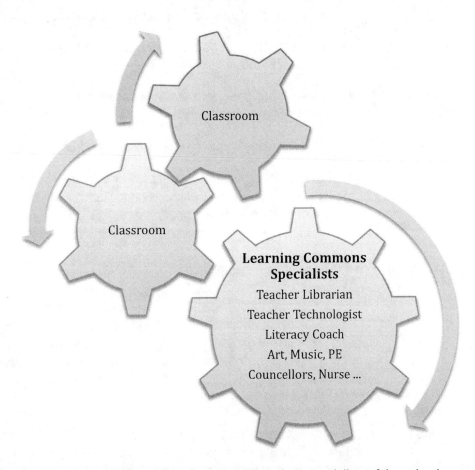

Instead of a single person in charge, one notices the various specialists of the school coming and going as they consult with individuals, small groups, and whole classes as they co-teach alongside the classroom teachers.

The types of activities co-existing simultaneously, is long and might include:

- A group of students gathering print and digital resources for a temporary classroom collection on a topic of study.

- A student team editing their own documentary on homeless persons in the school's neighborhood.

- A student technology expert seeking advice to work out connection problems to networks in the classroom.

- A classroom teacher and the music teacher who are helping learners compose original music for podcasts of their own stories.

- A class working with their teacher and teacher librarian to select both biased and unbiased resources on a controversial topic to be analyzed by the group.

- A single student linked into an online experimental study being done in the rainforest of Brazil.

- A small group of students having a brown bag lunch as they discuss the latest book in a fantasy novel series.

- Students in one corner receiving instruction from an artist in residence.

- Students in a conference room practicing for their poetry reading scheduled for the next day in the Commons during lunch and slated to be videotaped to upload to the community performance digital site.

The Experimental Learning Center

Constructed around teacher-centered principles, the Experimental Learning Center hosts professional development, experimentation, and exhibition of exemplary teaching and learning experiences in the school. Centered in this space that no one owns but everybody owns is the laboratory for testing new curriculum initiatives, experimental technologies, collaborative strategies, and cross grade-level or cross-curricular initiatives.

Governed by its own calendar, it draws upon the expertise of school, district, and outside experts and learner representatives who coach, do action research, and test new ideas for implementation throughout the school as a whole. Administrators walk through regularly to monitor initiatives and provide guidance and encouragement. This is the center of the school's professional learning community who are focusing on instructional improvements that deserve full implementation based on pilot testing.

The Experimental Learning Center is crucial to the orientation of new faculty members. Here they can consult the various subject specialists, teacher technologist, teacher librarians, coaches, counselors, and any other specialists serving in the school. The Learning Leadership Team may arrange job embedded staff development opportunities with outside experts. Other faculty may develop new technological skills, classroom management strategies, safety training, or perhaps refresher courses on legal responsibilities.

School-wide initiatives, projects, or grant writing happen here, as the faculty pulls together in a purposeful agenda for change and improvement. Issues across grade levels and disciplines such as literacy programs are planned, carried out, and evaluated. It is the learning laboratory of the school; a center of creativity, and innovation. Specific activities that might be happening at any given time in the Experimental Learning Center might include:

- Demonstration Lessons to model the teaching of student questioning skills to promote critical thinking across the curriculum.

- The district/board technical director (teacher technologist) meeting with the student tech team to teach them about new network procedures so that they can teach the protocols to the entire school.

- Writers of a new course meeting with the teacher librarian to select resources to meet the needs of all students.

- Teacher representatives meeting with a consultant via videoconference to plan an inservice day for the next month.

- The superintendent of school facilities discussing potential new policies with a class that has been studying vending machine usage across the district.

- Students writing in a blog environment are monitored and assessed for skill development, growth and fluency by the Literacy Learning Team and the classroom teachers.

The Virtual Learning Commons

Running simultaneously, 24/7/365 is the school's Learning Commons built by the students, teachers, learning specialists, and administrators with the two learning specialists, the teacher librarian and the teacher technologist as enablers and shadow leaders.

Like the physical space, the virtual space is constructed in two major configurations that constitute what the directors of technology might call instructional computing. This is quite different in nature from the administrative computing space where access is tightly controlled.

The Virtual Open Commons

The virtual space supporting the Open Commons is a very busy connection of projects, resources, tutorials, advice, repositories, as well as a tool source, assignment center, and a project production collaboration center. While there is a recognizable front page, this virtual space is a collection of links, sources, and projects being developed by learners, teachers, and learning specialists simultaneously. It may have originally been the library home page, but now it is constructed by the users who support each other in the overall learning community. Rules of behavior are supported and enforced by everyone. Various safeguards are in place to make the community functional and open to those who are working within its confines, including parents, partnering groups and schools, and anyone else who has a reason to be there.

Here, one might observe:

- Learners taking tutorials on how to cite various information sources in their productions and writings.

- Small groups in a class building a knowledge base on a topic they are studying.

- A team of learners uploading videos they have created to demonstrate to the faculty and students on how to upload their materials to the school's digital showcase.

- Learners taking online courses that could not be offered at their school.

- Teacher librarians preparing personal tip sheets that connect to teachers' assignments and uploading them to automatically appear on the home page of each student in a particular course.

- Virtual discussions of the latest award winning books in preparation for voting virtually in the state readers' choice awards program.

- A list constructed by a student club of best sources about bullying where they are asking for recommendations from others before they construct a school-wide policy.

- Areas where parents can collaborate as experts on various learning projects when they cannot be present in person.

The Virtual Experimental Learning Center

As the place where professional development, experimentation, professional learning communities, and learning initiatives are centered, this virtual space is communication central for learning improvement in the school. Announcements, calendars, and progress reports, plus the tools needed to support the ELC are located in the Center. This center provides the virtual glue that makes collaboration and school improvement work. It is constructed by the various leadership teams of the school—the administration, the faculty, and even district personnel—under the leadership of the teacher librarian and the teacher technologist.

At any given time, one might encounter:

- A group of teachers and learning specialists constructing a collaborative learning project, carrying it out, performing collaborative assessments, and reflecting on successes and challenges for the future.

- Administrators providing the first glimpses of a new statewide initiative that will be discussed with the Learning Leadership Team.

- Teacher librarians uploading a list of professional resources to a virtual chat space where the professional learning community can access them for an upcoming discussion.

- Schedules for an experimental classroom learning strategy that the entire faculty is invited to observe and reflect on as it progresses.

- The calendar of the ELC where all the learning specialists of the school can be invited and scheduled for collaborative development of learning activities by any faculty member.

- Announcements of local, state, and national conferences and professional learning opportunities.

- Grant opportunities for individuals, groups, and the school as a whole.

- Connections to major research, documents, forums, and other opportunities relevant to the focus of the individual school.

- Access to various assessment data sources of student performance.

When the virtual and real spaces are combined, then the total Learning Commons appears:

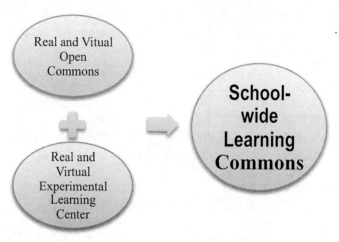

Checkup – Ask the Learners

If a visitor to the school were to randomly select a table during lunch and ask students about the role the Learning Commons plays in their school life, how would students respond? What sort of information would the students share? Perhaps something along these lines:

- **Environment** – A comfortable place where they can work, relax, learn, create or do.

- **Access** – A convenient, 24/7, source of materials, information, and advice they trust and contribute to.

- **Assistance** – They can comfortably obtain help from both adults and fellow students.

- **Personal Contributions** – They can voice opinions and give advice to assist in decisions about the construction of the Learning Commons. They have made contributions and feel some sense of ownership.

- **Experimentation** – They try new things, test technology or software, develop special projects, and see the adults doing the same.

- **Technology** – This is where you go to access and use hot new technologies and programs/software. The Learning Commons is the source of their connection to the digital world, and it is the center for discussion about that world and how they control it to their advantage.

- **Activities and Exhibitions** – They describe a variety of activities they have participated in or seen happening and know that many student productions are a part of the digital museum of the school.

- **A sense that adults coach and mentor them when they need help and that staff inquire about how they learn as well as what they know.**

- **It is a caring, supportive, place to learn without angst and pressure.**

In other words, the various learners recognize that the Learning Commons is a client-side organization where they have some say in what goes on and they are contributing as well as receiving as a user. They may not understand the impact that the Learning Commons is having on teaching and learning throughout the school, but they should recognize that they are engaged as they inquire, use, contribute, work and create.

Checkup – Ask the Teachers

Likewise, if a visitor to the school were to enter the teachers' lounge and interview random teachers about the Learning Commons, what sense of its value would be expressed? Perhaps something along these lines:

- **Environment** – as a part of their classroom – an extension of both work and learning activities; a model of environmental sustainability.

- **Access** – The source 24/7 of materials, information, and advice they trust and contribute to. That they can send individuals, small groups, and schedule the entire lass there as needed.

- **Assistance** – A place where they obtain help from both adults and students who are sharing their expertise.

- **Personal contribution** – They can voice opinions and give advice to assist in decisions about Learning Commons construction of. They have made contributions and feel some sense of ownership.

- **Experimentation** – A place to learn, test and share new strategies, test technology or software, develop special projects; the center of professional development.

- **Technology** – Recognition that the Learning Commons is the source of their connection to the digital world that extends into their classroom.

- **Activities and Exhibitions** – They remember and could describe a variety of activities they have seen happening and know that their student's work and productions are a part of the digital museum of the school.

- **Most importantly, they do not feel they are alone in the challenge of elevating every learner toward excellence. They are part of a teaching a learning team that merges classroom teachers and specialists in a mutual quest.**

In other words, teachers recognize the advantages of building and maintaining a client-side Learning Commons and feel at ease in the give and take of the idea of the Experimental Learning Center.

The Leadership Teams

A visitor might well ask: How has this all come about? What is the organizational structure that keeps it all running? In a prominent location, one might observe an organization chart similar to the one below that details the collaborative nature of a team of a school community:

The Learning Commons Partnership Teams

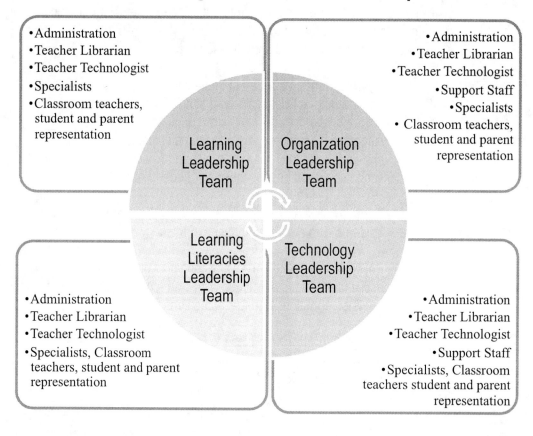

- Administration
- Teacher Librarian
- Teacher Technologist
- Specialists
- Classroom teachers, student and parent representation

Learning Leadership Team

Organization Leadership Team

- Administration
- Teacher Librarian
- Teacher Technologist
- Support Staff
- Specialists
- Classroom teachers, student and parent representation

Learning Literacies Leadership Team

Technology Leadership Team

- Administration
- Teacher Librarian
- Teacher Technologist
- Specialists, Classroom teachers, student and parent representation

- Administration
- Teacher Librarian
- Teacher Technologist
- Support Staff
- Specialists, Classroom teachers student and parent representation

This diagram is one example of the possible orchestration of a school leadership organization. Each school will need to design their own partnership structures based on school improvement goals and specific school needs. The triad of administration, teacher librarian and teacher technologist need to be the constant element for each team. Other specialist, support staff, classroom teachers, students and parents enrich the dynamics of each team with their particular expertise and interests.

The sense that the school is a learning organization becomes quite clear here at the center, the hub, the place of excellence. As we continue our tour we will examine program elements in the Learning Commons.

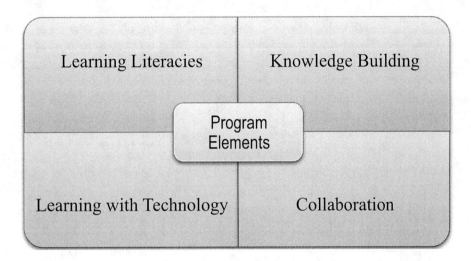

Scenario

- **It's Actually Happening.** In her annual report Joyce Valenza, teacher librarian at Springfield Township High School captures a moment in time in her center. 'Visitors to our library continue to note its energy, its spirit, and its coziness. During the video our students produced for the State Legislative Breakfast promoting school libraries, one student noted, "It's the closest thing we have to Starbucks" During a single block you will see students working in groups or independently as they create instructional videos, record podcasts, search scholarly journal databases, tell digital stories, present with our SmartBoard, write posts in curricular blogs, and collaborate using such on-line applications as wikis and Nings and Google documents. You will also see our students writing traditional papers and reading books and magazines."

Over to You. Discuss with Us at: http//schoollearningcommons.pbwiki.com

- Are there any features of your own school library or computer lab that pushes it over toward a client-side environment?

Knowledge Building
and the Learning Commons

In an inquiry approach to learning students actively engage with diverse and often conflicting sources of information and ideas to discover new ones, to build new understandings, and to develop personal viewpoints and perspectives.
(Ross Todd)

In both the Open Commons and the Experimental Learning Center, there is parade of learning units brought by classroom teachers to take advantage of various learning specialists and the rich resources and technologies available here. Whether experimental in nature or "mature" learning units, the focus is on inquiry based learning journeys. These journeys can be personal in nature, small-group projects, or whole-class learning experiences guided by the classroom teacher and one or more learning specialists. In the Experimental Learning Center, new ideas, strategies, experiments, and initiatives are being tested and modeled for the school. The major question is whether learners thrive better than with previous strategies. In the Open Commons, previously tested strategies are practiced on a regular basis.

For any of the learning specialists and, in particular, the teacher librarian, the curriculum of the specialist is being integrated with the learning standards required by the classroom teacher. This "just in time" and "need to know" instruction helps learners build their knowledge base and at the same time helps them learn even more efficiently. Examples might include how to judge the differences between fact and opinion as a political issue is being explored; how to think critically about conflicting media messages encountered on the topic; how to paraphrase by selecting major ideas in a variety of texts; and how to use a wiki to collaboratively build a case for a position the group is creating. As these learning journeys happen, the adults are watching, coaching, and assessing progress to insure that every learner either meets or exceeds the learning expectations. In other words, the Learning Commons supports a school-wide culture of inquiry fostering 'habits of mind' and 'learning dispositions' conducive to success.

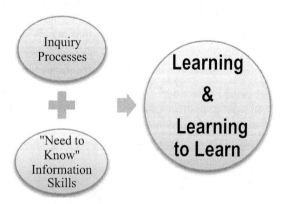

I'm smart and I can learn anything I want to learn!

Empowering the Learner

Inquiry in the Learning Commons is a dynamic learner centered process. Teacher librarians, other faculty and support staff provide 'just in time' and 'just for me' support and learning advice. Evidence of success includes:

As suggested by major foundational documents, learning becomes a quest; a journey. We can measure their success in this journey by considering the following indicators.

Doing

- Reading widely to build background knowledge
- Critically evaluating sources
- Applying inquiry processes
- Thinking analitically
- Using information legally and ethically
- Applying information literacy skills
- Tranferring technology skills to new applications
- Working with others

Learning to Learn

- Questioning
- Thinking critically and creatively
- Sorting information to make connections
- Analyzing information
- Communicating and collaborating
- Working with information and testing ideas
- Solving problems
- Making decisions
- Making connections to prior learning and experience

Knowing and Understanding

- Teaching others
- Empathizing
- Applying learning to new situations
- Understanding personal strengths and weakness
- Seeing the big picture
- Creating meaningful interpretations
- Envisioning next steps

Empowering the Teaching Team

As the classroom teacher and the learning specialists build and deliver these collaborative learning experiences, they are constantly assessing their own progress to ensure they are:

- Guiding and supporting **inquiry learning**

- Stimulating **critical** and **creative thinking**

- Building cross **curricular literacy** skills and **new literacies**

- **Engaging** and **effective**

- Empowering students to build **deeper understanding**

- Providing **knowledge building** learning experiences

- Employing a framework for designing **successful assignments**

- Effectively utilizing information and technology **rich learning environments**

- Providing **differentiated instruction** to ensure learning success for all

- Utilizing current technologies to **enhance the learning process**

- Stimulating excellent performance on both **formative and summative assessments** of either content knowledge or learning skills

Both the specialists and the classroom teacher follow the advice of W. James Popham[1] as they watch a learning experience unfold. He suggests four levels of formative assessment that monitor the learning experience as it happens.

1. Changing the structure of the learning experience if the learners are not building the subskills needed to accomplish the larger goal

2. Learners changing their learning to learn strategies as they progress through a learning experience.

3. The whole classroom/Learning Commons atmosphere changes to accomplish a particular learning experience and experiences over time.

4. Changes in the entire school climate as more effective strategies are developed along the way.

Knowledge Building in the Learning Commons

Because the Learning Commons has the richest resources and adult specialists available in the entire school, classroom teachers plan, schedule and assess learning experiences when they realize that two heads are better than one. The Learning Commons promotes an environment where every child or teen can flourish as a creator, investigator, critical thinker, or communicator. Using the principles of backwards planning promoted by Wiggins and McTigue in their *Understanding by Design*, teachers and learners can apply the Loertscher/Koechlin/Zwaan Think Models to push thinking far beyond the cut/paste/present tradition. The models find applications in both the Open Commons and the Experimental Learning Center depending on whether the learning units are being tried and tested or whether they have been adopted widely. The 18 models that stimulate high-level thinking are:

- **Background to Question Model**—where learners build enough background knowledge on a topic to formulate intelligent and engaging questions for themselves

- **Sensemaking Model**—where the learner takes a group of facts, ideas, or opinions and makes sense through visualization, classification, or synthesis

---

[1] Popham, James W. *TransFormative Assessment*. ASCD, 2008, p. 53.

- **Read, View, and Listen Model**—where learners read, view, and listen widely on a topic and combine what they learn with what others know

- **Advice to Action Model**—where learners consult a wide variety of advice and discern what are the wisest courses of action

- **Compare and Contrast Model**—where people, places, ideas, time periods, issues or solutions to problems are analyzed and compared to gain understanding of varying perspectives

- **Concept Jigsaw Puzzle Model**—where groups build expertise on subtopics and then combine their expertise to build a big picture across what everyone has discovered

- **Problems/Possibilities Jigsaw Puzzle Model**—where learners build expertise in various parts of a problem and then combine their expertise to solve the larger problem.

- **Decision Matrix Model**—where learners assemble facts, ideas, or opinions in a spreadsheet-type of matrix that enables them to do a comparative analysis in order to make an informed rather than a subjective decision

- **Patterns & Trends Matrix Model**—where learners assemble facts, ideas, or opinions in a spreadsheet-type of matrix that enables them to look for patterns or trends across the data collected

- **The Timeline Model**—where learners arrange ideas, events, or data in chronological order to enable comparisons, sequences, contrasts, or developments in order to see a larger picture of what is or what was happening.

- **History & Mystery Model**—where learners try to determine what happened, really happened, or find explanations to mysterious happenings

- **Take a Position Model**—where learners take positions based upon careful study rather than upon whim

- **Re-Create Model**—where learners create authentic reproductions whether literary, real, artistically, or creatively as possible

- **Reinvent Model**—where learners try to invent new ways of doing things, processes, environmental systems as close to the real world as possible

- **Learn By Doing**—where learners create apprenticeships, experiments, mockups, or performing tasks in the real or simulated world

- **Teacher-Directed Quest Model**—where learners do research projects under the teacher and learning specialist's direction such as:
  - Online Quest Projects
  - The Report
  - The Research Paper
  - The WebQuest as a Research Model

- **Learner-Directed Quest Model**—where learners take the initiative with adult shadowing of research projects such as:
  - Hero's Journey
  - Become an Expert
  - I Search

- **Mix It Up! Model**—where learners mix and match any of the models above

The Big Think – Building Collective Intelligence

For learners to reach the full potential of their inquiries they will explore the bigger impact of their work. Often these concepts and ideas are essentially those targeted in learning standards. As individual or group inquiries are completed and presentations given, learners realize that they have considerable expertise in the curriculum topic they have just explored. They have heard, seen, and experienced the findings of others and are ready to examine the collective knowledge of the class. The products or presentations are not the end of the inquiry project but the beginning of a Big Think. Learners take this opportunity to transform their learning into something new through collaborative knowledge building. They might:

- Conduct an active discussion about what they now know as a group vs. what they researched as individuals

- Attack a more difficult problem or challenge using the expertise of individuals to create an inventive solution

- Challenge the group with a new question requiring combined expertise

- Create a new question that leads them into the next learning experience

- Write about larger ideas and concepts learned by the group

- Collaboratively build charts, diagrams, maps, mind maps,

- plans, or action items based upon both individual and collaborative expertise

- Interact with an expert in order to compare what they have learned with what the expert knows about a topic and ways they might become experts themselves in various careers

- Take action on a problem or issue that surfaces during the learning experience

- Participate in related real world events that exhibits what they know, can do

The second part of the big think is to design an activity that will press students to think about the learning process they have just encountered. This activity could include reflection, questioning, and assessing techniques. A big think about the learning process should result in transference of skills and knowledge to other or new situations, self and peer evaluation, and goal setting. Together, they might:

How I Learn

How We Learn

How I Learn Better

- Develop a visual map of their learning journey and/or the information networks they used during the process.

- Chart individual emotions during the learning process on line graphs and layer the graphs to analyze for group or class patterns. Suggest learning tips for dealing with emotions, work habits, dispositions, and organization skills.

- Compare self-assessments and look for similarities or major differences. Use this data to set individual and class goals.

- Discuss and chart how their skill development applies to future work at school and in their personal lives.

- Explore careers that require inquiry process skills and begin a career database for future reference.

- Create a how-to presentation for another group of learners, e.g., best search strategies, note making techniques, presentation tips, etc.

- Develop questions to assess collaborative learning experiences and then develop criteria for better team work.

- Analyze the effectiveness of available time, resources, and equipment, and then prepare a needs assessment report for the Learning Commons.

- Reflect as a group: Are we getting better as learners? How can we learn more in less time? What technologies will help us learn better?

The third part of the big think is designed as a review by the teaching partners of data gathered from the learner, learning unit activities, and learning organization practices. Combined, this evidence will provide teaching partners with powerful data for refining or redesigning future learning experiences. See the EBP chapter for further details.

The bottom line is that the traditional end to a learning activity—passing in a paper, a project, or making a presentation—is now a springboard to keep the thinking and learning flowing.

The Learning Leadership Team

The school administrator, representatives of grade level or department faculty, student representatives, and learning specialists, including the teacher librarian, constitute the Learning Leadership Team. This professional learning community plans the professional development for the school, centers it in the Experimental Learning Center, encourages and promotes experimentation in the Center, and draws attention to exemplary teaching and learning in the Learning Commons and throughout the school. They conduct action research on experimental learning approaches, school or district initiatives, and guide assessment practices and progress toward achievement.

Kuhlthau, Maniotes and Caspari in their book: *The Guided Inquiry: Learning in the 21st Century* [2] describe the guided inquiry team as the group who:

- Understands the constructivist approach.

- Embraces the team approach to teaching.

- Includes administrators.

- Considers inquiry central to curricular learning.

- Commits to the development of information literacy.

- Allocates time for team planning.

- Defines clear roles for each team member.

- Designs assignments that enable and enhance inquiry learning.

- Allocates time for extended learning.

- Commits to guiding students through inquiry.

- Adopts a flexible approach.

- Endorses innovation and creativity.

The collegial relationships among team members that extend into the whole school faculty will be an important factor if experimentation and action research are to become part of the whole school culture.

---

[2] Kuhlthau, Carol C.,Leslie K. Maniotes and Ann K. Caspari.*Guided Inquiry:Learning in the 21st Century.* Libraries Unlimited,2007 page 60.

Systems and Networks that Support Learning and Experimentation

The Learning Leadership Team cannot operate in a vacuum. They require the resources to pursue initiatives, professional development, action research, and ongoing relationships with outside experts. Given these conditions the team affects the growth of the whole school as a learning environment that has its vision centered on long-term improvement rather than on short term dictates. The teacher technologist as part of the Learning Leadership Team provide the latest systems, hardware, software and support to facilitate the growth of knowledge building.

Scenarios

- **A Major Decision**. Every year, the sixth graders chose a location for a class excursion, but the teacher noticed that the decision was usually based on popularity and whim rather than sound decision making practice. Enlisting the support of the teacher librarian and the district technology coordinator, a research project ensued. Using a Google spreadsheet so that everyone could be working simultaneously, the students collected facts about specific locations on class-designed acceptability criteria: travel time, cost, fun factor, accessibility for all students etc. The teacher librarian taught not just how to find the answer to put into the spreadsheet but why accurate information was so very important. All three teachers became coaches. When the spreadsheet columns and rows were filled with data, the coaches asked the students what they should do now. The idea of reducing the size of the matrix developed, since any remote location, for example, would eliminate that excursion from consideration. Locations were eliminated until the last remaining were those that met all criteria. Accurate information and the process of decision-making were talked about over and over. They ended up confident that they had chosen the right excursion and they understood the basis on which good decisions are made.

- **A Big, Big Think**. When the state governor made a proposal to the regional state governors that they move on multiple fronts to work on the energy crisis, one school's science teacher thought that teenagers just might make a contribution. Mentioning the governor's idea, the science teacher suggested that the entire high school, and perhaps surrounding high schools could take on the governor's challenge. The school principal presented the idea at the first meeting of the professional learning community and there was a round of applause – let's do this from the entire faculty. Specialists, classroom teachers, community, experts, and excited students began the plans. The professional learning community demanded that the project be based on two major principles: careful research to produce deep understanding of the energy crisis, and a year-long reflection of the skills needed by the students that would enable them to make a sound contribution to a major problem. Thus began their journey. Every week rotating class reflections were scheduled: What do we know now? What skills do we need to advance further? What do you as a reader think could happen? And just why did they do metacognitive activity on a regular basis?

- **Action!** In a meeting of the professional learning community, the math teacher was warning that more attention be devoted to math in the school. The P.E. teacher noted that 9-year-olds needed more time with activities because of a major national study showing a drop in activity at that age, and, the teacher librarian demanded more time for the kids to connect to literature in order to raise reading scores. The technology director suggested to the group that all three competing agendas be combined into a single initiative. There was silence. Then, ideas! They named the project "Run a Chapter". A class committed to run daily while listening to a whole chapter of a book on MP3 players, taking and recording data of heartbeats before and after the run, then calculating individual performance, group performance and school performance as part of an effort to build understanding of applied math. Reflection sessions once a week did data analysis, discussions about math operations, principles of health, and of the stories they were listening to. The mayor was invited to the school for a tour by students of the entire project and he presented the students with a special fitness award at a final assembly of the year. He also passed out coupons the city recreation center for summer fun and the public library linked their summer reading program into the recreation center program.

- **Way Beyond all About**. The primary division in a remote rural school met with the teacher librarian to plan a unit on Cultures of the World. New books were ordered and appropriate video and web materials sourced. During a final planning meeting one of the teachers happened to mention a cool site she had just discovered where a primary teacher, Kathy Cassidy, was using a wiki and connecting with other classes around the world to reinforce math concepts. She shared the link http://primaryweb2.wikispaces.com/ and it sparked all kinds of ideas for learning with cultures, not just about them.

Over to You. Discuss with Us at: http//schoollearningcommons.pbwiki.com

- What experiences have you had with co-taught learning units between classroom teachers and specialists? What were the successes? The challenges?

- Have you had experiences with the Big Think at the end of a learning unit that helps learners explore both the collaborative intelligence of what they know, but also the metacognitive journey in getting there?

Resources

Foundational Ideas

- Sawyer, R. Keith, ed. *The Cambridge Handbook of the Learning Sciences*. Cambridge University Press, 2005.

- Popham, James W. *TransFormative Assessment*. ASCD, 2008.

Foundational Documents

- "Standards for the 21st-Century Learner," AASL. At:
  http://www.ala.org/ala/aasl/aaslproftools/learningstandards/standards.cfm

- "The Intellectual and Policy Foundations of the 21st Century Skills Framework,"
  Partnership for 21st Century Learning. At:
  http://www.21stcenturyskills.org/route21/images/stories/epapers/skills_foundations_fi
  nal.pdf

- International Information and Communication Technologies (ICT) Literacy Panel.
  "Digital Transformation: A Framework for ICT Literacy." Princeton, NJ: Educational
  Testing Services, 2007. At:
  http://www.ets.org/Media/Tests/Information_and_Communication_Technology_Litera
  cy/ictreport.pdf

- Anderson, Lorin W., David R. Krathwohl, and Benjamin Samuel Bloom. *A Taxonomy
  for Learning, Teaching, and Assessing: A Revision of Bloom's Taxonomy of
  Educational Objectives*. Longman, 2000. A revision of the popular taxonomy.

- Marzano, Robert J. and John S. Kendall. *Designing & Assessing educational
  objectives: Applying the New Taxonomy*. Corwin Press, 2008. An elaboration and
  restructuring of Blooms Taxonomy from a different perspective.

Professional Organizations

- Association for Curriculum Supervision and Development (ASCD)
  http://ascd.org

- American Association of School Librarians
  http://www.ala.org/ala/aasl/aaslindex.cfm
- International Society for Technology in Education
  http;//iste.org

- Canadian Association of School Librarians
  http://www.cla.ca/AM/Template.cfm?Section=CASL2

- Galileo Professional Network
  http://www.galileo.org/inquiry-what.html

- International Association of Learning Sciences http://www.isls.org/index.html

Professional Resources

- Blos, Susie and Jane Krauss. *Reinventing Project-Based Learning: Your Field Guide
  to Real-World Projects in the Digital Age*. ISTE, 2007.

- Callison, Daniel and Leslie Preddy. *The Blue Book on Information, Age Inquiry, Instruction and Literacy*. Libraries Unlimited, 2006.

- Danielson, Charlotte. *Enhancing Professional Practice: a Framework for Teachers*. 2nd ed. ASCD, 2007.

- DuFour, Rebecca, Richard DuFour and Robert Eaker. *Professional Learning Communities at Work Plan Book*. Solution Tree, 2006.

- DuFour, Richard, Rebecca DuFour, and Robert Eaker. *Learning by Doing: A Handbook for Professional Learning Communities at Work*. Solution Tree, 2006.

- Habits of Mind http://www.habits-of-mind.net/

- Jensen, Eric. *Brain-Based Learning: The New Paradigm of Teaching*. 2nd ed. Corwin Press, 2008.

- Koechlin, Carol and Sandi Zwaan. *Build Your Own Information Literate School*. Hi Willow Research and Publishing, 2003.

- Koechlin, Carol and Sandi Zwaan. *Info Tasks for Successful Learning*. Pembroke Pub. Ltd, 2001.

- Koechlin, Carol and Sandi Zwaan. *Q Tasks: How to Empower Students to Ask Questions and Care About Answers*. Pembroke Publishers Ltd, 2006.

- Kuhlthau, Carol C., Leslie K. Maniotes and Ann K. Caspari. *Guided Inquiry: Learning in the 21st Century*. Libraries Unlimited, 2007.

- Loertscher, David V., Carol Koechlin, and Sandi Zwaan. *Ban Those Bird Units: Thinking and Understanding in Information-rich and Technology-rich Environments*. Hi Willow Research and Publishing, 2005.

- Loertscher, David, Carol Koechlin, and Sandi Zwaan. *Beyond Bird Units: 18 Models for Teaching and Learning in Information-rich and Technology-rich Environments*. Hi Willow Research and Publishing, 2007.

- Tomlinson, Carol Ann, Kay Brimijoin, and Lane Narvaez. *The Differentiated School: Making Revolutionary Changes in Teaching and Learning*. ASCD, 2008.

- Marzano, Robert J. *The Art and Science of teaching: A Comprehensive Framework for Effective Teaching*. ASCD, 2007.

- Wiggins, Grant and Jay McTighe. *Understanding by Design*. Expanded 2nd ed. Prentice Hall, 2005.

- Zmuda, Allison and Violet H. Harada. *Librarians as Learning Specialists: Meeting the Learning Imperative for the 21st Century*. Libraries Unlimited, 2008.

Learning Literacies
and the Learning Commons

Learning Literacies

Reading
Writing
Listening
Communicating
Media Literacy
Visual Literacy
Information Literacy
ICT Literacy
Emerging Literacies

Defining literacy is a process of continuous negotiation that is fueled by social, economic and technological changes. To be literate is to have the skills and knowledge to make meaningful connections between what one knows and what one is trying to understand, apply, or communicate. The elastic definition of literacy now encompasses textual, digital, visual, media, informational, cultural and global under this broad learning umbrella. It could be argued that the umbrella literacy is now learning literacy and all of the above are nestled together. New literacies will continue to evolve as technologies appear and disappear and global and societal pressures shift the focus on specific information and learner needs. It isn't the label that is the critical issue, but the understanding of the need to bring Learning Commons into the 21st Century as evolving centers for literacy excellence.

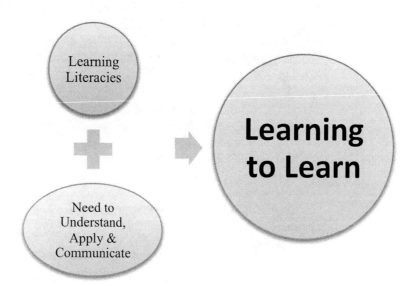

What is it that we want students as the rising generation to know and be able to do? Educators have developed content standards for every discipline and every grade level. Teachers and students are overwhelmed by the required content. Robert Marzano cites an analysis done by McCREL noting that if just the state content standards were actually taught, school would take 22 years to complete. Clustering expectations and examining existing curriculum for what Wiggins and McTighe term 'enduring understandings' is definitely needed. But the question remains, should it be content alone that drives our curriculum? Some organizations, as indicated in the chart below, have developed standards and processes to empower 21st Century workers and learners, not with the content to be mastered, but with the skills required to learn how to learn.

Toward A Definition of 21st-Century Literacies Adopted by the NCTE Executive Committee February 15, 2008

Literacy has always been a collection of cultural and communicative practices shared among members of particular groups. As society and technology change, so does literacy. Because technology has increased the intensity and complexity of literate environments, the twenty-first century demands that a literate person possess a wide range of abilities and competencies, many literacies. These literacies—from reading online newspapers to participating in virtual classrooms—are multiple, dynamic, and malleable. As in the past, they are inextricably linked with particular histories, life possibilities and social trajectories of individuals and groups. Twenty-first century readers and writers need to
- *Develop proficiency with the tools of technology*
- *Build relationships with others to pose and solve problems collaboratively andcross-culturally*
- *Design and share information for global communities to meet a variety of purposes*
- *Manage, analyze and synthesize multiple streams of simultaneous information*
- *Create, critique, analyze, and evaluate multi-media texts*
- *Attend to the ethical responsibilities required by these complex environments*
At: http://www.ncte.org/

Sample 21st Century Standards

Route 21	AASL	NETS for Students
• Information Literacy • Media Literacy • Critcal Thinking • Problem Solving • Creativity and Innovation • ICT Literacy	• Inqire, think critically, gain knowledge • Draw conclusions, make informed decisions, apply knowledge to new situations, and create new knowledge • Share knowledge and participate ethically and productively as members of our democratic society • Persue personal and aesthetic growth	• Research and Information Fluency • Critical Thinking, Problem Solving, and Decision Making •Creativity and Innovation • Communication and Collaboration • Digital Citizenship • Technology Operations and Concepts

These organizations are leading the way for educators to refocus student preparation for a changing world; a world where information is no longer the driving force. We have left the Information Age, where data and computer savvy ruled, and are now already immersed in a world of knowledge building and big Ideas. Preparing students with learning literacies is now paramount. By knowing how to learn students will be able to take informational content in any form and work it until they have deep understanding. They will know how to evaluate information and analyze it for relationships, discrepancies, perspectives, and bias. They will know how to use information and ideas critically and creatively to build personal knowledge, solve problems, and make decisions. The truly literate of the 21st century will have the knowhow to keep on learning, creating and sharing in spite of, or perhaps because of, the increasing complexity and challenges of information, technologies, and global issues.

Empowering the Learner

In the Learning Commons student learning experiences are designed to develop skills and strategies for dealing with a wide range of media, ever changing technologies, and vast amounts of information. Through relevant real world challenges they will develop learning literacies to mirror the changes brought about by the evolution of information and communication technologies. In other words, they will master the learning necessary to learn literacies that will help them master the content knowledge they are asked to learn. In simple terms, learners know a lot and they know how to learn anything they need to learn. Because the resources are plentiful and the technology accessible, as shown in the charts below, learners are developing skills for the purpose of using those skills to learn and, in turn, develop deep understanding. Learners may have mastered the skills of social networking for communicating with friends, but it is only when they blend them in the direction of their academic skills that they begin to develop the globally competitive skills they will need. The following chart identifies some of the indicators of the development of learning literacies.

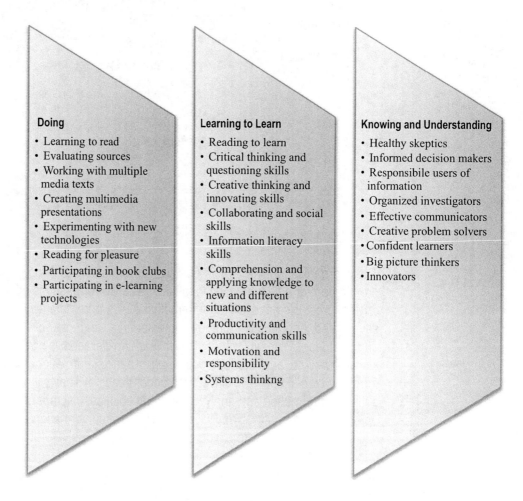

Doing
- Learning to read
- Evaluating sources
- Working with multiple media texts
- Creating multimedia presentations
- Experimenting with new technologies
- Reading for pleasure
- Participating in book clubs
- Participating in e-learning projects

Learning to Learn
- Reading to learn
- Critical thinking and questioning skills
- Creative thinking and innovating skills
- Collaborating and social skills
- Information literacy skills
- Comprehension and applying knowledge to new and different situations
- Productivity and communication skills
- Motivation and responsibility
- Systems thinkng

Knowing and Understanding
- Healthy skeptics
- Informed decision makers
- Responsibile users of information
- Organized investigators
- Effective communicators
- Creative problem solvers
- Confident learners
- Big picture thinkers
- Innovators

The Learning Skills Journey

We should explain to learners that a combination of learning to learn and subject content results in a journey that combines the skills and knowledge needed to propel them to success. Thus we are able to pass almost any kind of assessment thrown at us. We can pass a knowledge test of the topic at hand; we can also demonstrate our use of tools to help us be critical or creative thinkers; and, we can turn our knowledge into "doing" by exhibiting an action, a project, an action plan, or any other real-world event. As learners, we become more and more in command of our own learning; independent learners; and learners who appreciate and expect coaches, but have the ability to make progress ourselves. We can actually document our journey toward mastery and excellence and reflect regularly about whether we could be more efficient learners as shown in the following pathway:

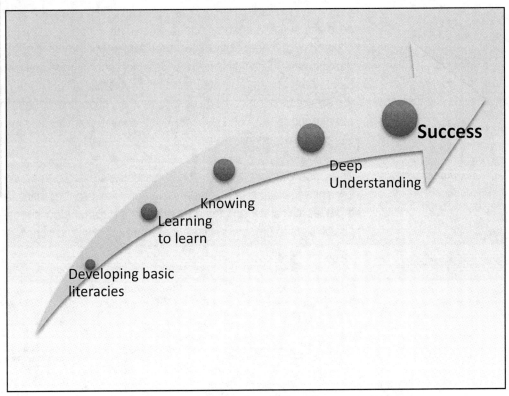

Learning Literacies Take Me on a Journey

Empowering the Teacher

During the last decade, much has been made about the need to raise basic literacy to prescribed minimal levels. The results have been less than spectacular. As Stephen Krashen[1] has said, today's youth read at about the same level as their parents did at the same age, but the problem is that the demand for literacy has risen. Coupled with the need to embrace more than just reading literacy, classroom teachers have felt intense pressure in spite of rising multilingual and continued poverty pressures.

Teachers at all levels have been urged to make the various literacies a part of their daily teaching routine, something that some secondary subject specialists have challenged. However, if progress is to be made helping learners exceed reading expectations and incorporating other literacies, then classroom teachers cannot be expected to succeed alone just because they are being told to do so.

---

[1] Krashen, Stephen. *The Power of Reading*. 2nd ed. Libraries Unlimited, 2006.

Empowering classroom teachers means that the entire school develops a plan and an atmosphere conducive to literacy excellence and that all the specialists work collaboratively to help achieve the goal. Teacher librarians supply every reader with a wide selection of materials the learners want to read and strive to develop a love of reading. Reading coaches work alongside classroom teachers both elementary and secondary to model and demonstrate the best strategies. Teacher technologist make wide reading far beyond the printed text appealing and available to learners. In other words, the school develops a reading culture in addition to emphasizing that it is just not enough to read at a minimal level, but there are numerous other learning literacies that are stressed.

The Open Commons is the space for all the literacies to be implemented. The Experimental Learning Center is the space where the entire faculty comes together to make literacies happen. The diagram below suggests some of the possibilities to empower all teachers through a whole-school sustained effort.

The Learning Commons as Literacy Central

The Learning Commons is the center of literacies because it provides the reason that every learner wants to become literate in contrast to being required to develop a minimal skill level. The Commons is at the center because it focuses on interest, excitement, engagement, and relevance as the central reason everyone wants to be literate because they want to be included. How does that happen? What transformation toward a client-side organization causes the switch from negative to positive? A starter list might include:

- The Commons reading collection circulates to every classroom and to every learner in unlimited amounts. Thus, access to what teachers want in their rotating classroom collections happens regularly. For learners, the Commons has what they want to read without restriction to the amount borrowed.

- The Commons is the center of reading and other literacy initiatives for the entire school. Amount read, viewed, and listened to begin with interest as the key factor and everyone becomes a critic of literature, film, Internet content, mass media, and the events surrounding new releases. Critical and fun discussions happen face to face and on every accessible Web 2.0 avenue.

- Learners research and develop exhibitions in a wide variety of media and, in the process, develop information literacy, critical thinking, creativity, and build expertise. Learners take pride in their creations because they are archived in the Commons and available to the world.

- Learners build skill in creating and using a wide variety of technologies that enhance the learning experience as well as help them communicate their knowledge across the room, across the school, or across the world,

- Learners build skill not just in printed text, but also in audio, video and mixed media during collaborative creations, projects, and events both locally, nationally, and globally.

- Learners know that no matter the culture, the skill level, the interest level, the language ability, the disability or the super ability, the Learning Commons is the cool place where what they need and want is in abundance. They feel ownership because they help build the collection. For teachers, it is THE ONLY place that makes the literacies possible when differentiated instruction is emphasized.

Participatory culture stresses the role of teens as creators, circulators, connectors, and collaborators--rather than simply consumers--of media. Young people participate in the creation and circulation of media content within social networks that extend from their circle of face-to-face friends to a larger virtual community around the world. Our central goal is to engage educators and learners in today's participatory culture. It is our belief that young people need to both make and reflect upon media and in the process, acquire important skills in team work, leadership, problem solving, collaboration, brainstorming, communications, and creating projects.

http://newmedialiteracies.org

Given the underlying policies that support literacies in the Learning Commons, visitors who spend time there might list the following as evidence that literacies are being transformed into knowledge building:

- A team of students deconstructing advertising samples to identify techniques that were used to deliver a message.

- A class learning how to experiment with graphs to effectively represent the data they have gathered on recycling in their community.

- A group of English learners viewing a movie version of a piece of literature and reading graphic novels of the piece in order to get the basics of the story in their heads before attacking the full text in English.

- A class surfing the web to find authoritative sources on an issue they are studying and building their own "trusted" list to use in their next research session.

- The technology teacher coaching a group of students on use of a new camera as they make a video tutorial for other students.

- The fantasy book club having a brown bag lunch in simultaneous discussion with the same club in a different school across the city.

- A class talking with an invited expert comparing what they know with what the expert does in real life.

- A group of students leaving for the local bookstore where they are choosing graphic novels based on selection criteria they have developed.

The Learning Literacies Leadership Team

The Learning Literacies Leadership Team of the school has student representatives and solicits a variety of advice from all the learners of the school as everyone contributes to the construction of the policies and practices of the Learning Commons. Administrators, classroom teachers, and specialists, including the teacher librarian, constitute this leadership team. A sense of inclusion keeps both teachers and students confident that they are contributing, sharing, and working collaboratively. It is a professional learning community that involves its clientele. Together the team will:

- collaboratively build a print-rich environment for students
- Promote and celebrate the reading habit
- Timetable sufficient time for free voluntary reading
- Design learning experiences to focus on reading for meaning
- Empower students to develop their own learning lifestyle
- Utilize technologies to *build* literacy competencies
- Integrate cross curricular learning literacies

- Apply information literacies to knowledge building
- Collaborate to explore and experiment with new literacies
- Facilitate job embedded professional development
- Observe, track and analyze growth of learning literacies across grade levels and disciplines
- Support action research projects (individual and collaborative)
- Review, reflect, redesign literacy initiatives
- Make literacy fun and irresistible.

Systems and Networks that Support Learning and Experimentation

The system that will sustain a literate and learning community begins with a vision by the entire leadership team of the school. Rather than a one-size-fits-all model or a top-down initiative, a purposeful collaborative is needed to make a sustainable change. The walls between the old library, the computer labs and the classroom must crumble as client side policies replace command and control. Everyone understands the needs of the learners because they have a voice. The classroom teachers embrace the specialists of the school in the massive literacies initiatives. The system accepts the notion that literacy is not dictated but is an integral part of fascinating learning activities that motivate the learners to build the skills they need to participate. Excellence rather than minimums is the focus.

The Experimental Learning Center is the place for the documenting of school-wide initiatives. Data walls demonstrate progress of the experimentation and the initiatives currently under way. It becomes one more place around which to unite the entire faculty in school improvement.

Scenarios

- **Book Bags.** In a poor urban neighborhood, languages were diverse and reading scores in the basement. The school literacy team met to consider what they could do to address this major problem. The teacher librarian who was in graduate school to get her masters, had heard in class of the success of the book bag program. She convinced her peers to try it. The district library department was anxious to help, so they purchased enough red canvas bags for all kindergarten and first grade students in the school and were able to find some funds to purchase high interest books for this age group. Each month, each class would come to the library and the children would select two books for their book bag; one they could "read" themselves and one that could be read to them. The bags were numbered and every day, the classroom teacher would send a bag home with each child and it would come back the next morning, to be exchanged with a fresh one. At ten books read per week, each child was reading 300-500 books a year. Book loss was miniscule. Reading scores jumped. The book bag program became a mainstay of the entire reading initiative.

- **SSR with a Twist**. A high school chemistry teacher complained to the teacher librarian that SSR time was wasted time in his classroom and he was going to recommend that it be discontinued. The teacher librarian suggested they try a fresh approach. Taking the topic about to be studied by all the beginning chemistry classes, the pair pulled all the related, "fascinating" books from the library collection, borrowed interesting books from the public library, and used the library credit card to purchase duplicate copies of a few titles from the local bookstore as well as science journals. The students helped find interesting topic related on-line articles. Every day for the first week, the teacher and the teacher librarian introduced a few new items to the class and modeled the SSR time with the students saving the last five minute of SSR to share what they were reading and invited students to trade ideas and books. SSR became a popular activity again and general background knowledge was increased.

- **Blog to Write.** The literacy coach was arguing for more opportunities for middle schoolers to write and the students had lost interest in doing quick writes. The teacher technologist, the teacher librarian offered to work with the eighth grade language arts teachers to infuse new life and interest in writing. First, they polled the reading interests of the students and then introduced the idea of forming book clubs and blogging about what they read. Every student was invited to join and assist with an interest blog: motorcycles, makeup tips, true survival, movie-book tie ins, and fantasy were the most popular first blog topics. The students, with the help of the teachers, and specialists, collected books and passed them around. They read during SSR time and blogged after every free reading SSR period. Club topics and bloggers changed monthly under the student leadership team. All the adults assumed coaching positions in the initiative. The literacy coach and teacher technologist had teams of kids create some short videos giving writing tips for "selling" a book to another person on the blog. A reading community and writing community emerged.

- **Going Green**: The principal attended the specialists' professional learning community and asked what they could do to push the school's going green initiative. A brainstorming session with students, faculty, parents, and community experts generated a slogan for the project as well as a long list of initiatives. The students on the committee were intrigued with the idea of getting the message out so they asked their teacher technologists for help. She showed them examples of different kinds of media formats. Their teacher librarian connected them with media literacy websites where they discovered how they need to consider their message, their audience and match that to the best format. A production team went into full swing and what began as a school project to save energy, developed into a major student-produced media blitz of the community as well.

- **Role Models.** Several reports of harassing and bullying of students on social networking sites led to demands from the parent council for action. The Health specialist invited the police department into the school to consult with staff and to provide workshop material for student awareness sessions. A comment made by the police officer clicked with the teacher librarian and technology teacher. The office said that on the social networking sites that young people frequent, there is often misbehavior and inappropriate mimicking because they only have each other as role models. Adults do not tread in these spaces. The specialists had failed in their efforts to encourage teachers to use blogging with students in spite of all the evidence they had gathered that showed how engaged students are on the read/write web. They now proceeded to help teachers see the contributions they could make by providing good role models as well as some parameters for social networking. Blogs were set up with social networking skills and behaviors embedded for those interested. Teachers were amazed by the amount and quality of free writing their students were spinning on the blogs, especially students who normally say very little in class. They are being bombarded with inquiries about other ways they can share on their class blogs.

Over to You. Discuss with Us at: http//schoollearningcommons.pbwiki.com
- How does a school connect reading skill with fun?

- How are learners building their reading skill through non-traditional media?

- How can all teachers help develop literacies no matter their subjects taught or grade level?

Resources

Foundational Ideas

- Anderson, Lorin W., David R. Krathwohl, and Benjamin Samuel Bloom. *A Taxonomy for Learning, Teaching, and Assessing: A Revision of Bloom's Taxonomy of Educational Objectives.* Longman, 2000. A revision of the popular taxonomy.

- International Reading Association http://www.reading.org/ See their many policy statements on reading and literacy.

- Marzano, Robert J. and John S. Kendall. *Designing & Assessing Educational Objectives: Applying the New Taxonomy.* Corwin Press, 2008. An elaboration and restructuring of Blooms Taxonomy from a different perspective.

- National Council of Teachers of English. Various statements on literacies for children and teens, at: http://www.ncte.org/

- National Council of Teachers of English. *Standards for Middle and High School Literacy Coaches: A Project of the International Reading Association in Collaboration with NCTE, NCTM, NSTA, and NCSS, and with support provided by Carnegie Corporation of New York.* NCTE, 2005. Just one of the various standards documents published by NCTE. See their website for a complete list at: http://www.ncte.org/

- *National Educational Technology Standards for students.* 2nd ed. ISTE, 2007.

- Jenkins, Henry, *et.al.* "Confronting the Challenge of Participatory Culture: Media Education for the 21st Century." MacArthur Foundation. *at:* http://www.projectnml.org/files/working/NMLWhitePaper.pdf

Professional Organizations

- National Council of Teachers of English (NCTE)http://www.ncte.org

- Association for Supervision and Curriculum Development (ASCD) http://ascd.org

- American Association of School Librarians (AASL) http://www.ala.org/ala/aasl/aaslindex.cfm

- International Society for Technology in Education (ISTE) http://www.iste.org/

- International Reading Association http://www.reading.org/

Professional Resources

- Braunger, Jane and Jan Patricia Lewis. *Building a Knowledge Base in Reading.* 2nd ed. NCTE, 2006.

- Calliso, Daniel and Leslie Preddy. *The Blue Book on Information Age Inquiry, Instruction and Literacy.* Libraries Unlimited, 2006.

- Fogarty, Robin. *Literacy Matters.* 2nd ed. Corwin Press, 2007.

- Harvey, Stephanie and Anne Goudvis. *Strategies that Work: Teaching Comprehension for Understanding and Engagement.* 2nd ed. Stenhouse 2007.

- Ivey, Gay and Douglas Fisher. *Creating Literacy-Rich Schools for Adolescents.* ASCD, 2006.

- Kajder, Sara. "Reaching the Reluctant Learner," *Educational Leadership*, v. 65, no 6, March, 2008.

- Koechlin C. and Zwaan S. *Build You Own Information Literate School.* Hi Willow, 2006.

- Krashen, Stephen. *The Power of Reading.* 2nd ed. Libraries Unlimited, 2006.

- Ohler, Jason. *Digital Storytelling in the Classroom: New Media Pathways to Literacy, Learning, and Creativity.* Corwin Press, 2007.

- Warlick,David. *Redefining Literacy for the 21st Century.* Linworth Publishing, 2004.

- Warlick, David his blog at: http://davidwarlick.com/2cents/

Technology
and the Learning Commons

The Learning Commons is the space where learners and technology converge. This merger creates a dynamic environment where world class learners blossom. There is general agreement that learners who are astute in the wise use of technology have a better chance of competing globally. For schools, the challenge is not only to create the networks, acquire the software, and make both operational, but to react to the transformative influences of technology on the way everyone learns.

"The prevailing technologies of a particular place and time have always been intimately linked with education, because a society's tools are both the subject and the means of its learning. Today, the fact that technology pervades almost every sphere of life – from home to work to play – results in profound implications for learning, both in schools and throughout life. Students are able to connect – and create – with their peers, and with the wider world, in ways that were unfathomable just a few years ago. Learning tools – media, telecommunication, and networked technologies coupled with learning science – are rapidly evolving into a powerful support system for acquiring the skills needed for modern life."[1]

Technology and Systems + Need to Understand → Learning and Constructing Knowledge

Administrative and Instructional Computing

It is important to make a distinction between administrative computing in the school and instructional computing. Administrative computing is a tightly controlled space for budgets, schedules, student records, grades, and anything else related to administration. Security for this system is essential.

The instructional computer system that serves the teaching and learning function in the school is quite different from the administrative system. The instructional system is constructed cooperatively. It is a virtual learning community consisting of many different commercial tools, open sources, Web 2.0 applications, and perhaps Web 3.0 virtual worlds. This space is built on the Google Model of information systems; the "If *they* build it, they will use it." The

---

[1] The Intellectual and Policy Foundations of the 21st Century Skills Framework http://www.21stcenturyskills.org/route21/images/stories/epapers/skills_foundations_final.pdf, p. 5-6.

learning community may access this community through district servers, but is more likely to be a distributed model where various functions are "in the cloud." This means that the actual servers could be anywhere but are accessible through a home page linking the various applications together.

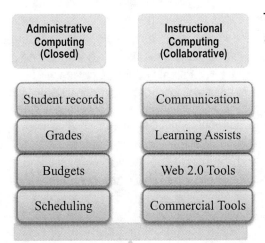

The trend for Web 2.0 applications is toward more and more secure areas that only a teacher, specialists, invited students, and invited parents can access. Most importantly, these systems are available 24/7/365. District and school teacher technologists, regularly facilitate and participate in creating, experimenting with, using, and assessing the impact of the various tools on learning. As members of collaborative teaching and learning teams, teacher technologists focus on access, usability, and learning results. They also research emerging technologies while promoting the creative and clever combinations of current technologies.

Interestingly, while separate, both systems inform each other as administrative computing responds to what is happening in the instructional side and vice versa. For example, low cost web 2.0 tools might replace expensive commercial applications, thus reducing budgets. Likewise, the various student performance data in the administrative system is used by the learning literacies leadership team to recommend instructional changes.

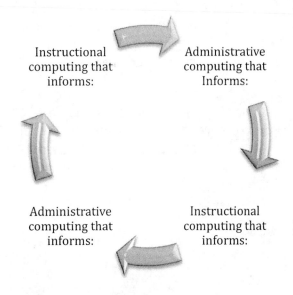

The Learning Commons as Learning Tech Central

The Learning Commons is the center for instructional computing in the school. Everyone feels a sense of ownership while participating in a perpetual beta experiment. For learners, the sentiment is that technology, as an extension of themselves, empowers them to know, do, and understand. To the teachers, technology enables strategies that help them reach every learner and propels the possibilities for achievement far beyond what could be expected in a traditional environment.

The Learning Commons is an open, wireless environment enabling computing devices of various types to be connected instantly. Moveable furniture allows for different configurations of teaching or learning groups without regard to connectivity restraints at designated places. As one-on-one computing becomes a reality, a single, uniform, device will be replaced by devices of personal preference with robust capabilities.

Technology in the Learning Commons is not only the latest and most extensive, but it has a reputation for reliability. Its many options of formats, media, research, production, and communication possibilities enable individual learning styles and needs. This is the center for support, experimentation, troubleshooting, and sharing of expertise.

Like many computer stores, students, adults, staff and volunteers serve at the Commons expert bar, where technical advice on both hardware and software is available. Students who staff the expert bar might extend their volunteering into industry-standard expertise and licensing.

Student content and products are not only created, but also uploaded for assessment and easy display to other students, parents, and perhaps beyond the school networks. Thus, the Learning Commons is not only the production center for demonstrations of current learning (exhibitions, portfolios), but it also serves as museum and archive, as well as an assistive instructional space open to discussion and input from the outside world.

Empowering the Learner

What is it that technology does for the learner that cannot be done without it? In experimentation of technology in the Learning Commons, the focus is on strategies that build the capabilities of the learner. What are these strategies and characteristics that boost learning? What is the advantage in learning how to build a personal information space and learning to manage oneself in that space?

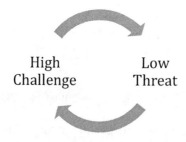

High
Challenge

Low
Threat

Rather than focus on the networks, devices, and applications, attention is squarely on what the technology does to help students know, do, understand, and become a better learner as illustrated below.

Doing
- Enables sharing and communication of content, projects, and performances
- Lets me experiment and do projects in real, simulated, and virtual worlds
- Allows me to accomplish more with enlarged impact
- Be active in the solution to issues and problems

Learning to Learn
- Encourages me to create
- Enhances problem solving
- Enables me to build my own information spaces
- Provides opportunity to build hardwared and software tool skills
- Enhances inquiry and mastery
- Promotes efficiency
- Allows collaboration worldwide

Knowing and Understanding
- As an extension of my senses
- By extending my experience
- Helping me build background knowledge
- Learning more collaboratively than by myself (collective intelligence)
- Permitting me to engage in larger and more complex conversations
- Provides new opportunities to see the big picture and larger perspectives
- Valuing my contribution

At the beginning of each school year, learners should build or re-build their own information space using a tool, such as iGoogle, that allows them to take control of the interface between themselves and the world of the Internet. This process continues as learners progress. Loertscher and Williams, in their book *In Command*, demonstrate the various layers of a student's information space. Learners first build a personal information space containing tools and information they need to survive each day—calendars, to do lists, assignments from teachers, RSS feeds, and essential software applications. To this space they add other self-designed pages from group projects, specific classes requiring lots of attention, and even an entry point into the world of the Internet. This constructed space allows them to function in an organized fashion without the overwhelming overload of the entire Internet. Learners are in command, in control, and prepared to succeed at school, at home, or in extra-curricular activities. In cooperation with teachers, teacher librarians, tech specialists, and parents, learners set up the filtering system for their site based on their own responsibility index. Thus, their filter is like a dimmer switch or a rheostat, moving more open or more closed as needed.

Learners use their information space as the foundation to construct their own personal learning system where they are interacting with people, information and ideas. Interestingly the learner begins to develop various learning spaces for the different projects and activities of life thus they have their personal network system for their daily routines, another for their reading hobby network, a third for a local history project team and yet another for gaming. Each of these has a support system of not one but many learning commons, organizations, experts and tools. This facilitates user control of what is usually the overwhelming juggernaut of the Internet.

At the same time they are becoming, reflective, responsible users of the wired world. Learners must gain the skills and the wisdom to govern their own behavior and identity in digital spaces. They will discover an online digital extension of themselves and explore who they really are. Some studies indicate that behavior can be quite different in the many emerging environments beyond who one is in school, at home, or with friends. Professionals are there to guide the development of positive characteristics such as responsibility, congeniality, and other ethical behaviors.

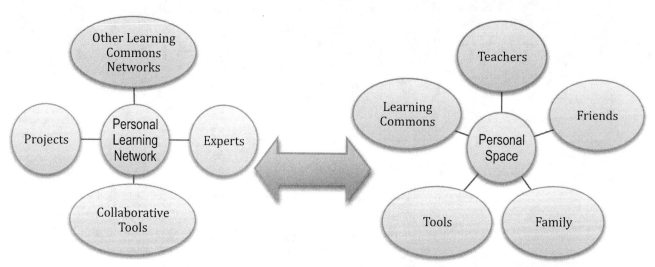

The learner created information space is continually evolving as skills and technologies change. Most importantly, students will need to learn how to succeed using this constructed space. They will need to consider:

- What familiar tools will I be able to use?

- Which new tools will enhance my learning and who can help me apply them?

- How do I bring new information to my attention?

- What do I need to know to create, store, and share my learning?

- How will I begin to confront the many voices trying to get my attention?

- Who is saying what to me, for what reasons, when, and for what gain?

- What are the ethical challenges of functioning successfully in digital space? How do I avoid such problems as plagiarism?

- How do I stay safe in digital worlds?

- How can I use the tools available to me to be better organized, more efficient, and more creative?

- How will I update the skills I now possess?

- How can I use the social networking skills I already have to enhance my academic success?

Confronting such questions while constructing personal information spaces helps learners prepare to function in the new, real world of technology and to become competitive in that world.

The U.S. Federal Trade Commission has recently published its guide for kids and teens with the slogan: Stop. Think. Click[2] with its seven practices for safer computing:

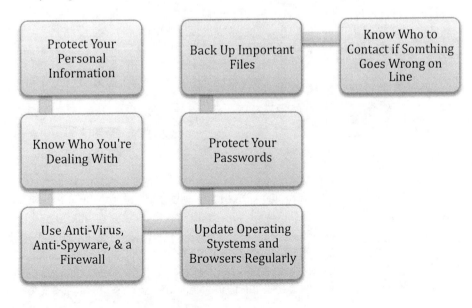

2 http://onguardonline.gov/stopthinkclick.html

Empowering the Teacher

The major question each teacher faces is how technology can help each of the learners in my care toward excellence? Until technology becomes a real extension of myself rather than just equipment or networks to battle, that question remains unanswered. Each teacher in the school is provided with opportunities to use technology in ways that improve their own performance and job satisfaction. To do this, each teacher asks the question, "What is the impact of technology on my teaching?" Based on the possibilities for improvement, the technology leadership team provides the support necessary to make those possibilities a reality.

How can Technology Impact Teaching?

Enhancing Teaching Strategies	Maximizing Learning Opportunities	Management of Learning	Personal Growth and Development
• Access to experts both near and far • Improved presentations • Monitoring results as teaching progresses • New methods of presentation beyond the lecture • Extending possibilities for differentiation • Opportunities to collaborate with teaching colleagues	• Instant communication with learners and caregivers • More options in the kinds of choices I can provide learners • Both synchronous and asynchronous • Time to reflect before resonding • Empowerment through valued voice • On demand and repeatable	• Paperless communication, assignments, and grading • A variety of ways to assess, document and analyze learning • Simplifying assessment practices • Tracking student attendance and progress	• Online professional development • Participation in action research studies across subjects and schools • Instant access to professional literature • Connections to professioanl learning communitities in the school and beyond

The Learning Commons is the laboratory where the faculty and staff learn and develop their skills in embedding technology to boost learning and achievement. Classes, short courses, and students manning the expert bar provide support to those seeking to improve their skills. Collaborative experimentation with teacher learners and commons staff not only happen and are refined in the Commons, but are also exhibited to other faculty observers who wish to improve the role of technology in their own classrooms.[3] Through collaborative experimentation creative new uses of technologies emerge.

Small teams of students can receive training in various software and hardware applications and then fan out to teach other students and faculty throughout the school. Professional development activities can be taught either by adults or students who have the expertise. The collegial model of "I teach you, you teach me, and we succeed together" becomes the motto of such improvement initiatives.

Performance indicators from the NETS Standards for Teachers[4] can be used to document progress as teachers:

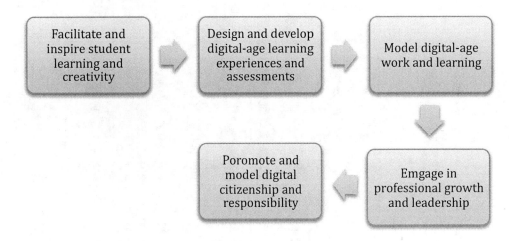

Systems and Networks that Support Learning and Experimentation

Because the Learning Commons is a learning laboratory, teacher technologists continually experiment with networks, open source applications, and Internet access to facilitate rather than restrict learning. We strive to create a read, think, write, reflect, web filled with personal learning spaces and networks. These networks are never static; they are ever evolving test beds of innovation. Access and responsibility is tested in the Commons and then introduced to the students and the school as a whole. Both students and teachers, test and experiment with new software applications for recommendation on a wider scale.

---

[3] such sentiments about technology and the need to improve both access and professional development are echoed in: *Access, Adequacy and Equity in Education Technology: Results of a Survey of america's Teachers and Support Professionals on Technology in Public Schools and Classrooms.* NEA and AFT, May 2008. At: http://www.nea.org/research/images/08gainsandgapsedtech.pdf

[4] *National Educational Technology Standards for Teachers.* 2nd ed. ISTE, 2008, p.9.

Building an instructional network requires that the system itself be a teaching and learning resource constructed not only by teacher technologists and teacher librarians, but by the users themselves. We no longer think of completing the construction of a physical network, rather the network becomes organic; a perpetual beta. It is true that as the uses of the network evolve dysfunction occurs causing disruption and frustration however that is the nature of progress.

The Learning Commons Collaborative Help Center

Sharing Center for Teachers	Sharing Center for Students	Sharing Center for Caregivers
• Professional learning opportunities • Links to tools and tutorials • Action research reports • Helpful sources for teaching ideas • Extended hand of support	• Homework help links • Assignments and pathfinders • Book discussion groups and recommended book, movie, and music lists • Helpful tutorials • Tools and applications	• School initiatives • Advice for supporting learners • School discussion groups/ parent groups • Calendars • Ways to monitor progress

Safety concerns coupled with the threats of legal challenges often are used as barriers to the opening of instructional networks. In a client-side organization, the learners will help construct the safety nets and review them on a regular basis. The adults not only coach young people how to stay safe crossing the street, on the playground, or in the neighborhoods, they do so in virtual space. Thus, the adults leave nothing to chance as they educate, educate, and educate. They realize that unguided interaction will surely result in likely catastrophe. There is no such thing as a totally safe or legal-free physical or virtual space, but there are many ways to handle the problems encountered.

The school library website becomes the collaborative Learning Commons help center with drag and drop applications, resources, RSS feed recommendations, and other helps that can be brought on to the student's or teacher's personal information space. It is also the space for conversation, communication, and collective knowledge building.

The system has open and closed areas of access to the general public on a need to know/participate basis.

One of the challenges of building systems is the undue pressure by commercial organizations to sell expensive systems and packages based on the Microsoft model to school districts or schools. If a client side system is to

48

be built and supported, then great care needs to be taken in the selection and implementation of packages that may or may not be what users would embrace and use. Such purchasing decisions should be within the province of the Technology Leadership Team as described later.

Technology and Learning Virtually

More and more opportunities exist for learners to take part of their coursework or all of it through virtual learning networks. The ideas and principles of the Learning Commons apply in virtual spaces just as they do in physical spaces. Specific courses should be a part of the Learning Commons activities and receive support and collaboration from the mentor teachers and specialists in the school just as regular classes would have. For virtual schools, these organizations should have their own virtual Learning Commons as described here. Teacher technologists and teacher librarians build the commons as a collaborative between teachers and learners to allow both synchronous and asynchronous delivery. We aim for anytime, anywhere, anybody access.

Assistive Technologies

Everyone needs assistive technologies. We all require an Internet connection to see e-mail, the human eye cannot see viruses without electron microscopes, the visually impaired require audio assistance, and GPS helps us to navigate in unknown territory. Since everyone needs assistive devices the stigma of help for a few disappears. Cost is not always the major factor but a range of choices for the learner is essential. The primary understanding is that everyone helps everyone else achieve by overcoming whatever barriers exist. When assistance becomes a normal part of the learning environment, everyone benefits.

The Technology Leadership Team

School administrators establish a leadership team to guide the technological systems, the applications, and the impact of technology on learning. This professional learning community has representatives from both adult and student users. Collectively they hold a shared vision as they advise the administration on implementation opportunities, problems, and budgets, and assess the impact of technology on the school as a whole.

Scenarios

The Geek Team. One computer teacher we know assembled a "cadre of student geeks" in her computer club. Every few weeks, the club met to learn a new application or jointly share troubleshooting for applications already in use around the school. This teacher advertised to the faculty that if they had any trouble, to call on any member of the geek club. A few tried it; some teachers were reticent because a student might uncover the teacher's own incompetence; but, after a month or so of successes, the news got around the faculty that the geek club was a stunning success. It was a tipping point from fear of technology to the attitude, "You teach me; I'll teach you; and we will all succeed together." Such an attitude change in one area may be the stimulus toward a collaborative attitude in other areas, turning an isolated and competitive faculty into a collegial professional learning community.

Reinventing What We Already Own. Jeff Brown of Kawartha Pine Ridge Board of Education, Peterborough, Ontario, Canada, the Instructional Leadership Consultant for Technology and Learning Resources, regularly uses videoconferencing systems to facilitate administrative, school board meetings, classroom enrichment and collaborations with classes and individuals around the world. When he discovered a deaf student, who is bound to his wheel chair and isolated because few around him could sign; the idea came to use the existing technology to link the deaf around the province together. Using a computer based video conferencing system this student meets with other students every Monday to discuss personal and curriculum based topics. For them it is a chance to speak and have their thoughts heard and their ideas valued by being part of a real time conversation.

The individuals in this community talk together in American Sign Language. A new community was born. The smiles on the faces, the depth of discussion and the development of personal connections are enabled by the technology. Our young man, who lost his hearing over time, has experienced a rebirth in his citizenship in society based on his access to technology and innovative thinking.

Connectivity Entitlement Agreement (CEA). In support of access to the powerful learning tools on the Read Think Write Web, learners need to have guidelines within which to work. Typically these rules are laid out in Acceptable Use Policies, which outlines the limitations and the consequences of any contravention of the policy. These documents are command/control and protection based.

Learners using the network resources, often test the effectiveness of the security established on networks that these punitive documents are established to protect. Savvy learners are often challenged by these restrictive documents like a red flag as they have no vested interest in the network. In response to this Kawartha Pine Ridge District School Board in Ontario Canada is developing a Connectivity Entitlement Agreement (CEA).

The CEA is designed in such a way as to outline the relationship of the learners in the board with the network resources offered by the board to augment learning. Individuals are extended access to resources within a wired world.

The mindset shift here is, as a member of a greater learning community, each member has rights to use the network and the collective responsibility to maintain its functionality to honor the rights of others. In this way the learners have a vested interest in the continued operability of their link to the world.

Over to You. Discuss with Us at: http//schoollearningcommons.pbwiki.com

- How do we as schools and districts move into the safe but open Web 2.0 instructional computing environment?

- What is the impact on achievement and engagement when learners discover the power of transformative technologies? As this happens, what happens to the way teachers teach?

Resources

Foundational Ideas

- "Digtial Transformation: A Framework for ICT Literacy: A Report of the International ICT Literacy Panel." Educational Testing Services, 2007. At: http://www.ets.org/Media/Tests/Information_and_Communication_Technology_Literacy/ictreport.pdf A major theoretical document that formed the foundation for the creation of an ICT assessment by ETS.

- "The Intellectual and Policy Foundations of the 21st Century Skills Framework." At: http://www.21stcenturyskills.org/route21/images/ stories/epapers/skills_foundations_final.pdf A white paper arguing the intellectual foundation of technology and learning.

- Jenkins, Henry, *et.al.* "Confronting the Challenge of Participatory Culture: Media Education for the 21st Century." MacArthur Foundation. *at:* http://www.projectnml.org/files/working/NMLWhitePaper.pdf

Professional Documents:

- Partnership for 21st Century Skills. Route 21. At: http://www.21stcenturyskills.org/route21/ A model of what skills young people need to have and be able to do to be competitive globally.

- "Standards for the 21st-Century Learner." AASL
  http://www.ala.org/ala/aasl/aaslproftools/learningstandards/standards.
  cfm A vision document that integrates technology into the inquiry
  process.

- "Children and Electr4onic Media" Vol. 18, No. 1 of *The Future of
  Children*. Princeton-Brookings Institute, Spring, 2008.

- *"National Educational Technology Standards for Students."* 2nd ed.
  ISTE, 2007. (available from ISTE)

- *"National Educational Technology Standards for Teachers."* 2nd ed.
  ISTE, 2008. (available from ISTE)

- *Digital Transformation: A framework for ICT Literacy: A Report of the
  International ICT Literacy Panel."* ETS, 2007.

Professional Organizations:

- International Society for Technology in Education (ISTE) with its
  NETS standards and annual NECC conference provides a great deal
  of guidance for technology programs.

- Most jurisdictions have a professional organization connected to
  technology with an accompanying annual conference.

- Check out opportunities in local and national organizations to exhibit
  technological projects and creations like science fair competitions.
  Available at:
  http://www.futureofchildren.org/usr_doc/Media_08_01.pdf

Other Resources

- Pitler, Howard, et. al. *Using Technology with Classroom Instruction
  That Works.* ASCD and McREL, 2007.

- Blos, Suzie and Jane Krauss. *Reinventing Project-Based Learning.*
  ISTE, 2007.

- *Educational Media and Technology Yearbook.* Annual. Libraries
  Unlimited.

- Hendron, John G. *RSS for Educators: Blogs, Newsfeeds, Podcasts,
  and Wikis in the Classroom.* ISTE, 2008.

- Jonassen, David H., et. al. *Meaningful Learning with Technology.*3rd Edition. Prentice-Hall, 2007.

- November, Alan. *Web Literacy for Educators.* Corwin Press, 2008.

- Simonson, Michael, et.al. *Teaching and Learning at a Distance: Foundations of Distance Education.* 4th Edition Prentice-Hall, 2008.

- Spector, J. Michael and Philip A. Harris. *Handbook of Research on Educational Communications and Technology.* Routledge, 2007.

- Warlick, David. *Classroom Blogging.* 2nd Ed.Lulu.com, 2007.

- Rose, David and Anne Meyer. *Teaching Every Student in the Digital Age.* ASCD 2002.

Blogs
- Warlick, David. 2¢ Worth: Teaching & Learning in the new information landscape... at: http://davidwarlick.com/2cents/

- Heppell, Stephen. Stephen Heppell's Weblog at: http://www.heppell.net/weblog/stephen/

- November, Alan. November Learning at: http://novemberlearning.com/index.php?option=com_frontpage&Itemid=1

- McKenzie, Jamie. From Now On: the Educational Technology Journal at: http://fno.org/

- Jukes, Ian. The Committed Sardine at: http://web.mac.com/iajukes/thecommittedsardine/BLOG/BLOG.html

Collaboration
and the Learning Commons

The establishment of the Learning Commons as a community of learners opens the door for more effective instruction and, consequently, school improvement. Here we experience many types and layers of collaboration - everyone working together to analyze and improve teaching and learning for all. Teachers and administrators work on specific facets of school improvement and safety. Students work with other students and teachers on solving problems, building knowledge, and creating together. The broader school community works within the Learning Commons to support learning and local initiatives. All work together supported by the rich resources and technologies of the Commons.

The school library has a long and successful history of improving student achievement through collaboration. Research has consistently shown that in schools where the teacher-librarian and the classroom teacher collaborate to design, teach and assess learning experiences together, test scores are consistently higher.[1] Based on that experience, the Learning Commons provides a 'tipping point' for building successful collaborative teams.

Learning Teams + Critical Collective Questions → Learning and Learning to Learn

Empowering the Learner

Students work with partners or in groups on projects, they coach others, they read to buddies, they plan with staff, they consult experts, and they network utilizing evolving technologies in the Commons. As they work and play collaboratively, students are

[1] Lance, Keith Curry and David V. Loertscher. *Powering Achievement*. Hi Willow Research & Publishing, 2004.

54

learning and honing needed skills for school and life. The following are sample indicators of collaboration:

Doing
- Group work
- Literature circles
- Information circles
- Discussion, debate
- Peer evaluations
- Group reflection
- Coaching peers
- Active listening

Learning to Learn
- Networking
- Communicating
- Problem solving
- Decision making
- Fexibility
- Responsibility
- Inquiry

Knowing and Understanding
- Sharing expertise
- Collaborative knowledge building
- Learning by teaching
- Developing multiple perspectives
- Developing points of view
- Empathizing with others
- Conceptualizing big ideas
- Sharing with diverse audiences

Empowering the Teacher

High-level collaboration means that the classroom teacher and one or more specialists co-teach a learning experience. This means that together they:

- Combine the goals and objectives of both partners for the learning experience.

- Create a joint assessment, both formative and summative.

- Plan and then co-teach the learning activities.

- Conduct a high-level "so what" activity that extends learning.

- Jointly assess the learners.

- Reflect together on their successes and challenges.

- Report their results and impact on learners.

- Plan for further collaborations as a part of evidence-based practice.

The goal of a true collaboration is to demonstrate that "two heads are better than one." Collectively, teachers and specialists have been able to achieve better results than if they had taught separately. By combining their creativity and expertise, they have rediscovered the joy of teaching. Together, they have had more success reaching every learner.[2]

Other levels of collaboration, such as cooperation, support, encouragement, and the sharing of good ideas across the faculty, grade levels and departments are practiced in the Learning Commons. The result is a healthy learning community, a functional whole, a school that is achieving its mission.

Benefits of Collaboration

Collaboration and working in teams is a major idea in the social and business worlds. Web 2.0 technologies have given birth to huge collaborative projects (folksonomies) such as Wikipedia, LibraryThing, Flickr, and del.icio.us. Such projects build knowledge bases tagged by many, searchable by everyone. In business, collaborative teams who solve problems are becoming the norm. Accounts of and guides to such collaborations are in the popular literature in such books as:

- *We are Smarter than Me: How to Unleash the Power of Crowds in Your Business*

- *Wikinomics: How Mass Collaboration Changes Everything*

- *Group Genius*

- *Developing Group Genius: Getting the Most out of Group Decision-Making*

- *Linked: The New Science of Networks*

- *Convergence Culture: Where Old and New Media Collide*

The benefits of collaboration are well known in the learning communities where they exist and are touted in the professional literature. Yet, the benefits are elusive to many, particularly when test score pressures create a competitive rather than collaborative environment or where traditional methods are entrenched over time. The literature of leadership in school reform places the challenge of change squarely on the shoulders of the administrators of the school who must begin with a vision and use sound principles in the building of a school leadership team. Often, the leadership team of the Learning Commons adopts the well-know practices of successful professional learning communities. Dana and Yendol-Hoppey[3] list the following ten essential elements of healthy inquiry-oriented PLCs:

1. A vision that creates momentum for their work.
2. Build trust among group members.
3. Pay attention to the ways power can influence group dynamics.

---

[2] Collaborative units are reported and you may add yours at http://www.davidvl.org under the action research tab.

[3] Dana, Nancy Fitchtman and Diane Yendol-Hoppey. *The Reflective Educator's Guide to Professional Development: Coaching Inquiry-Oriented Learning Communities*. Corwin Press, 2008, p. 21-47.

4. Understand and embrace collaboration.
5. Encourage, recognize, and appreciate diversity within the group.
6. Promote the development of critical friends.
7. Hold the group accountable for and document learning.
8. Understand change and acknowledge the discomfort it may bring to some PLC members.
9. Have a comprehensive view of what constitutes data, and are willing to consider all forms and types of data throughout their PLC work.
10. Work with building administrators.

Using this list of essential elements, what benefits are likely to emerge and should be documented? The following chart lists a few; make a list of your own.

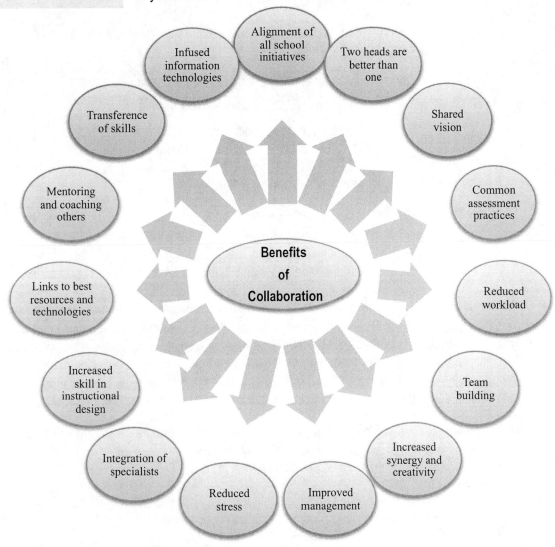

The Learning Commons as Collaboration Central

It does not take a genius to observe a healthy collaborative atmosphere in the Learning Commons. Parents, school board members, outside visitors, and, in particular, the students and teachers of the school sense what is going on at almost any hour of the day. They sense the dynamics of the Center, the enthusiasm and the purposeful nature and engagement of environment. They can question almost anyone in the school who is involved and supportive of what goes on there.

Learning together is the mantra of the Learning Commons. Some examples of collaboration are:

- A group of teachers meeting with the teacher librarian to plan a learning unit.

- Learners from several classes planning for a visiting expert with the assistance of a guidance counselor.

- A group of learners and community leaders meeting online to plan events for Black History month.

- Learners, teacher librarians, and teacher technologist in two different school districts collaborate on developing a Healthy Lifestyle campaign.

- The reading coach meeting with grade level representatives to set in motion the state literature choice voting for the next year.

The Learning Commons Partnership Teams

The number of leadership teams needed in any one school will vary. In this book we have suggested that the Learning Leadership Team, the Learning Literacy Team, the Organizational Leadership Team, and the Technology Leadership Team are key groups to the building and the propelling of the Learning Commons to provide improved learning for all. We suggest that all teams should work through the frameworks established in the Experimental Commons and the rich resources and support of the Open Commons to conduct the important work they do for the benefit of all teachers and students. The consistency of working through the same channels will help align real progress that can be analyzed and sustained. Principals and other school leaders can find and track all initiatives in one place as opposed to hunting down isolated and often factious 'start and stop' programs all over the school.

Regardless of the mandate, all collaborative learning teams work together with a set of collective inquiry questions critical to the common vision of improving learning for all. For example: those developed by DuFour, DuFour and Eaker:[4]

- What is it our students must learn?
- What is the best way to sequence their learning?

---

[4] DuFour, Rebecca, Richard DuFour and Robert Eaker. *Professional Learning Communities at Work Plan Book*. Solution Tree, 2006, p. 8.

The challenge confronting a school that has engaged in the collective consideration of a topic is answering the questions, "So what?" and, "What, if anything, are we prepared to do differently?"

DuFour, et.al. Learning By Doing. Solution Tree, 2006, p. 111.

- What are the most effective strategies to use in teaching this essential content?
- How will we know when they have learned it?
- How will we respond when they don't learn?
- What will we do when they already know it?
- What can we learn from each other to enhance our effectiveness?

Systems and Networks that Support Learning and Experimentation

Collaboration is one of the most discussed ideas in the professional literature but often the least practiced. As authors, we have heard from teacher librarians a plethora of reasons why it does not happen:

- Collaboration is not taught to preservice teachers.

- Tradition has one teacher in a closed classroom.

- Teachers don't know how to collaborate.

- Scheduled classes allow no time to collaborate.

- The principal does not encourage it.

- Teachers treat specialists such as the teacher librarian as support personnel rather than colleagues.

- Teachers feel that if they collaborate, others will discover their weaknesses.

- Tradition: "I have always done it this way. Just leave me alone. I have too much to cover."

- Collaboration takes up too much valuable time.

Kuhlthau, Maniotes, and Caspari[5] provide a similar list of inhibitors but also suggest enablers:

---

4 Kuhlthau, Maniotes, Caspari . *Guided Inquiry – Learning in the 21st Century*. Libraries Unlimited, 2007,
    p. 51-52

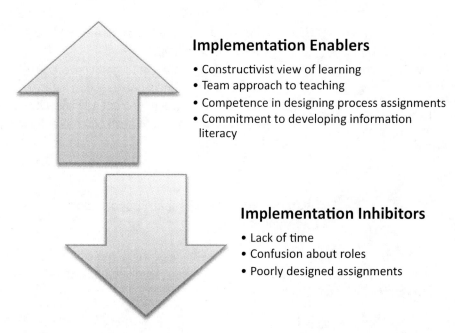

Implementation Enablers

• Constructivist view of learning
• Team approach to teaching
• Competence in designing process assignments
• Commitment to developing information literacy

Implementation Inhibitors

• Lack of time
• Confusion about roles
• Poorly designed assignments

Obviously, a system that stimulates collaboration is a leadership issue that begins with the principal and the school's leadership teams. Turn negatives into positives with a set of well-known strategies that will be the center of focus for the school leadership teams to confront directly. Consider:

- Replacing dysfunction with purpose
- Isolation with teaming
- Locked doors with an open doors
- Specialists shunned to specialist inclusion
- Rigidity with realistic flexibility
- Habits and predispositions with transformation

The list of resources at the end of this chapter provides direction in this transformation.

Scenarios

- **Movement and Learner Collaboration**. A classroom teacher faced a group of middle schoolers, many of whom were English learners and came from various ethnic backgrounds. Noting the lack of trust for any cooperative learning, the teacher happened to mention this problem to the teacher librarian. The teacher librarian recommended that the PE teacher become involved because of the new standards for physical education recently published by National Association for Sport and Physical Education or NASP. In a planning meeting together, the classroom teacher, the PE teacher, and the teacher librarian decided to do a prelude movement exercise with the learners before the teacher and the teacher librarian presented the collaborative project. All three teachers joined the leaner's in the gym the first day of the unit where the PE teacher taught the kids to get on the floor and tie themselves in a large human knot and then figure out how to get out of the knot without letting loose of their hands. Their experiment with the learners made it possible to approach learner collaboration for the first time. (ed. note: Watch the entire video at: http://www.edutopia.org/new-physical-education-movement-video

- **A Day in the Life of.** The year-end tests were over. Two weeks remaining in the school year. The students were chomping for vacation; the teachers left wondering how to survive the bored and restless. In the last professional learning community meeting, everyone faced the grim reality of babysitting. The technology specialist rose to the occasion and suggested that the entire school do a "Day in the Life of" project. The teacher librarian seconded the motion; other specialists said they'd help and in fifteen minutes, dread was replaced with creativity and excitement. Calls to the community went out instantly and a massive brainstorming session with adults and the students ensued. Oral histories; podcasts; photo essays; research; video tours, and any other media they could muster was used. Interviews were conducted in a full day followed by days of group refinement of projects. The next to the last day of school was an evening community program and docent tour of the neighborhood via gallery walk. The last day was class reflections. What do we now know? What should happen to all our documentation? What problems did we notice in our community that need to be solved? In a fifteen-minute secret, reflective meeting of the specialists, the feeling was unanimous that the cement doors of the classroom had crumbled.

- **On the Right Foot.** When the principals in the district were asked for their plans for staff development, one principal set forth the idea that every new teacher to the building should have one less class to teach the first semester. Instead of the class, the new teachers would have their release time at the same period of the day and would meet once a week with the teacher librarian and the technology specialist with the balance of the days used to build units of instruction and receive other training they needed. The resulting collaboration was incredibly successful and began to affect teacher retention immediately.

- **Spotlight.** The principal wanted to highlight a successful instructional practice, linked to research, during the monthly faculty meetings. She did not want to turn the presentation into a political reward system, so she called in the technology specialist and the teacher librarian and asked them to assist. They were to observe an instructional practice, during the month and make a five-minute presentation, but not identify the teacher observed. This pair of specialists decided to make it a flashy, glitzy, and humorous, but pithy comment on quality teaching and learning, particularly collaborative experiences. What they found was that after the presentation, several teachers thought they were the ones being spotlighted. It was a pleasant beginning to a meeting usually packed with administrivia. Gradually collaboration increased and teaching and learning became more exciting and more meaningful.

- **Study, Study, Study.** With only two weeks left before final exams a couple of students who like to study together decide to check out the school library website to see if anything is there to help them. They were surprised to find a great deal of support; links to study tips, and essay writing as well as subject specific links. They rediscovered all the projects they had done this year in the library as well as the accompanying Pathfinders and the links to project wikis and blogs. Reviewing the collaborative project sites gave the students an idea and they immediately started to explore how to set up a virtual study group space. Within a few minutes, they were all set and ready to invite others into their Exam Think space.

Over to You. Discuss with Us at: http//schoollearningcommons.pbwiki.com

- How will collaborative learning experiences prepare students for their future in the 21st Century?

- How can schools build on the successful collaborative experiences in school libraries to create school wide PLCs?

- What are the present roadblocks to collaboration and how can we overcome them?

- How will collaboration help teachers redesign and implement more effective teaching and learning strategies?

Resources

Foundational Ideas

DuFour, Richard, Rober Eaker, and Rebecca Dufour, eds.. *On Common Ground.* National Educational Service, 2005.

DuFour, Richard, Rebecca DuFour, Robert Eaker, and Thomas Many. *Learning by Doing.* Solution Tree.2006.

Professional Organizations

- Association for Supervision and Curriculum Development (ASCD)
  http://ascd.org

Professional Resources

- Blankstein, Alan M., Paul D. Houston, and Robert W. Cole. *Sustaining Professional Learning Communities*. Corwin Press, 2008.

- Fullen, Michael, Peter Hill and Carmel Crevola. *Breakthough*. Corwin Press, 2006.

- Fullen, Michael. *The Six Secrets of Change: What the Best Leaders Do to Help Their Organizations Survive and Thrive*. Jossey Bass, 2008.

- Gregory, Gayle H. and Lin Kuzmich. *Teacher Teams That Get Results: 61 Strategies for Sustaining and Renewing Professional Learning Communities*. Corwin Press, 2007.

- Hord, Shirley M. and William A. Sommers. *Leading Professional Learning Communities: Voices From Research and Practice*. Corwin Press, 2008.

- Lance, Keith and David V. Loertscher. *Powering Achievement* 3rd ed. Hi-Willow Research and Publishing, 2005.

- Villa, Richard A., Jacqueline S. Thousand, and Ann I Nevin. *A Guide to Co-Teaching: Practical Tips for Facilitating Student Learning*. Corwin Press, 2008.

- Wild, Monique D., Amanda S. Mayeaux, and Kathryn P. Edmonds. *TeamWork: Setting the Standard for Collaborative Teaching, Grades 5-9*. Stenhouse and NMSA, 2008.

- Williams, R. Bruce. *More than 50 Ways to Build Team Consensus*. Corwin Press, 2008.

Other Resources

- Cameron, Greg, Monette McIver, and Roger Goddard. "A Different Kind of Community," *Changing Schools*, Winter, 2008. Download at: http://www.mcrel.org/product/339. The only thing missing from this essay is the role that specialists could have as an integral part of a collaborative faculty working to improve their school.

- Library Research Service http://lrs.org/ is a source for evidence linking library media programs to achievement.

Building the Learning Commons
as a Client Side Organization

Creating a Learning Commons can be both an evolutionary and a revolutionary organizational transformation. It might be triggered by a change in staff, a grant opportunity, a change in administration, or even an Ah Ha! moment in a professional learning community conversation. Using any catalyst, the conversation centers on the transformation from an "organization centered" concept into a client side model where both students and teachers win. It is the difference between the "If you build it, they will come" model to the "If *they* build it, they will use it" model. It transforms bored students into engaged and productive learners; teachers from masters to coaches.

Beginning with the concept of the Open Commons and the Experimental Learning Center, a combination of learning tools and learning sciences contributes to a fresh and exciting learning environment. Central to this concept is the notion of world-class excellence. The Learning Commons is, as much as possible, a product of client input. Shadow leadership and coaching help clients move from their own, often minimal, expectations toward a more ambitious vision for themselves.

To be successful, this initiative will need participation, "buy-in" and collaborative vision building that capitalizes on the strengths of both the adults and students to provide all the opportunities needed to succeed. Such a change places the client first and should not be a short-term solution, but rather a long-term sustainability model. The vision is one of a "perpetual beta" idea where change is keeping pace with the evolution of the post-industrial society. To the learners this means that the school not only gives them the support and tools to learn but also empowers them to capitalize on their abilities. For the teachers, the opportunities offered by this organization allow them to keep improving, as they enjoy the benefits of job embedded professional development.

Creating an Organization That Empowers the Learner

What kind of organization empowers the learner rather than corrals everyone into the same user mode? What structure defies the one-size-fits-all mentality? The organizational team of the Learning Commons should brainstorm ideas that push from regimentation to opportunity. A sample list might include:

- Totally flexible spaces in the Learning Commons vs. a fixed space configuration.

- User preferred devices vs. prescribed connective devices.

- Inclusion of elastic print and digital resources vs. only static materials collections.

- Multiple professionals, support personnel, and volunteers vs. single adult consultant.

- Accessible yet safe instructional computer systems; centralized systems to open source; and distributed systems vs. limited and tightly controlled networks.

- Learner-constructed information spaces vs. central library web sites constructed without user input.

In any of these transitions, learners need to be involved in the design and ongoing development. Insight into many key ideas will come from student experiences in social networking and with current trends, as various industries such as; music, movies, messaging systems, and television evolve and appeal to the younger set. *Involvement, choice, engagement,* and *differentiation* are all terms that will be considered as policies and procedures develop. Care must be taken to build systems for various types of learners with different ability levels, learning styles, languages, and cultural backgrounds.

Creating an Organization that Empowers the Teacher

The legendary idea of academic freedom (when the door closes, I do what I darn well please) coupled with intense pressure to raise each learner to a minimal level of achievement has isolated the classroom teacher and contributed to the high dropout rates of not only teens but also their instructors. Numerous autobiographical accounts of the overwhelming challenge, particularly the first year teacher, brings to mind Frank McCourt's memoire, *Teacher Man,* as he faces the overwhelming task of making a difference alone. "Just close the door. No help, sorry. Just keep them under control."Faced with overwhelming odds, few teachers can share a success story like *Freedom Writers,*[1] or, *Educating Esme'.*[2]

The Learning Commons, as the center of school improvement, offers a lifeline from the frustration often expressed in the teacher's lounge. Administrators will focus the entire faculty on excellence as they lead the initiative of continuous experimentation and improvement. "You are not alone. Here's a lifeline. We are all on the journey together."

The first year teacher is an obvious place to begin in the construction of the Experimental Learning Center. Here, they are introduced to their lifelines: the materials, the resources, the systems, and the specialists that will become their safety net. Panic, negativity, and stress are counterbalanced with collegial understanding, sharing, and encouragement.

Alongside first year teachers, the more experienced who already possess attributes of flexibility and creativity will be likely first candidates for the activities featured in the

---

[1] "Freedom Writers" the movie. Also a book: *Freedom Writers Diary.*
[2] Raji, Esme'*Educating Esme': Diary of a Teacher's First Year.* Algonquin Books, 2001.

Experimental Learning Center. As success is achieved with this group and as evidence of improved achievement surfaces, others will climb aboard. The Learning Commons as Organization Central.

Traditional approaches to every aspect of the previous library and computer laboratory need to be re-examined. Often it requires that we do a mirror image vision of what has normally been the case; a 180 degree rethinking. In the graphic below are listed various component parts of the Learning Commons organizational elements followed by a brief description of each of those elements coupled with some rethinking:

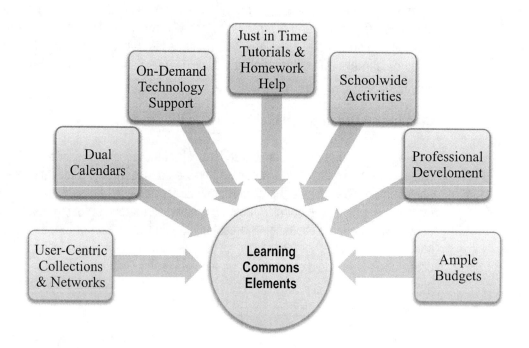

- **User-Centric Collections.** Both teachers and learners participate in the growth and development of resources. High quality information resources are not free as often supposed. Ample budgets provide access to copyrighted materials. Combined with the best of the free resources, the collection is available 24/7/365 to all users. These resources include online databases, on demand instructional video, textbooks, and the tutorials needed to utilize those resources. Materials spanning various reading levels, cultures, interest levels, and genres are sufficient to surround both the learner and teacher with a plethora of choices given any quest. Physical items such as books rotate from the Learning Commons into the classrooms and into the homes of learners all year around. The concept of ownership of resources often is replaced by "access to," meaning that collections are elastic in nature rather than static. In-house collections are linked to collections all over the world such as art museums, great libraries, government sources, and document repositories. The Learning Commons contains the formats, the genres, the types of media, and the devices needed to use the resources wherever and whenever the user needs them. Digital and physical collections will evolve at the preferences of the users.

- **Dual Learning Commons Calendars.** The Open Commons and the Experimental Learning Center are each governed by a separate calendar. All specialists and assigned administrators are scheduled through the Experimental Learning Center as needed. This includes the teacher librarian whose first responsibility is to the improvement of instruction rather than tending and managing the Open Commons. For the most part, the Open Commons is the province of support personnel under the direction of the teacher librarian. This could be said of any specialist in the building who has a "warehouse" to supervise besides a teaching and consultative role to the faculty at large. Specialists can also be calendared virtually as well as in person. For example, a teacher technologist might be scheduled in the ELC three periods a day and teach in another space the rest of the day. The more flexible the calendar, the more the various specialists are able to collaborate to maximize both the classroom teacher's agenda as well as their own in raising achievement.

- **On-Demand Technology Assistance.** Effective instructional computing systems require that the users have access to various types of hardware and software that assist them in learning. While we can equip learners with numerous devices and systems, regular tune-ups are needed to keep the various systems operational. Such tune-ups are the responsibility of everyone. I help you; you help me; and we all keep it running and operational. Instead of one-size-fits-all protocols, everyone is developing expertise to deal with and handle problems that arise. Cadres of learners and teachers are trained to address problems and then are expected to spread their knowledge. Both faculty and cadre members staff the expert bar in the Open Commons to assist individuals or small groups who are struggling with technology or software. These mini-experts are recognized in their various classes as sources of information and help. Disaffected students are often enticed by the need to help to become more connected to the learning community. Hackers can turn around to be systems designers and troubleshooters. Such assistance extends from the Learning Commons into the classrooms and also into the homes as suggested in the following section.

- **Just-in-Time Tutorial and Homework Help.** The idea that if I am stuck and there is usually someone around to help whether during school hours or after hours is a sign that client side practices are working. Help centers for doing homework both in person and via technology are very common. However, help for technology, software, and the various literacies such as information literacy are often not common. As a part of the Learning Commons website home page, everyone participates in building the help center of that site which can then be drawn down by individual learners into their own information space as needed. The idea that there is one expert in the school who provides timely assistance is unthinkable and undoable by even the most organized. Engaging everyone to help everyone else promotes collaboration across the entire learning community. For example:

- A team of students could devise a quick tutorial on how to create and use iGoogle to build their own information space.

- Help links are available on common problems in searching the Internet and on ways to get exactly what you need.

- Pathfinders to help everyone in the class find the right information for a particular assignment quickly, are created collaboratively.

- **School-wide Activities.** The Learning Commons is a great place to center all school-wide initiatives from reading promotions, fund raisers for the entire school, accreditation projects, to grant writing activities and implementation. Like business and industry, teams can be formed for each of the various initiatives that have a finite life and are reconstituted as opportunities arise.

- **Just-in-Time Professional Development.** As the center of professional development, action research, and other experimentation, the Experimental Learning Center (ELC) becomes the center for school improvement. Programs for first year teachers, curricular changes, outside consultant programs, professional learning community meetings and activities, and any other training programs emanate from the Learning Commons and are scheduled on the ELC calendar. Because the Learning Commons is the center of resources and technology, it is a natural place to integrate the potential of information and information technology into whatever training is being proposed, experimented with, or pushed out into the various classrooms or departments. The ELC is often like a fishbowl where visitors may observe, critique, interact with, examine, and test before various programs radiate out into the school as a whole.

- **Ample Budgets.** How much does it cost to provide the materials and technological devices for each learner? Budget an allocation to equip each learner with a tech device each year including its updates, repair, and replacement. Add to this the cost of materials such as books, video, online databases, and subscriptions to e-resources such as digital books, podcasts, or other materials accessible via digital devices. Begin by budgeting the equivalent of an average textbook per student per year and follow the impact of those expenditures on individual learners and their usage patterns.

- **Financial Efficiency.** The Learning Commons is the place to maximize spending power, a place where competition is centered, and commercial vendor monopolies are resisted. Instead learners, teachers, teacher librarians, and teacher technologists advocate for, select, implement, and hold accountable the very best resources and technologies that are required to support every learner.

The Learning Commons Partnership Teams

Leadership in the Learning Commons is team-based rather than centralized in a single individual. Each school begins with the functions desirable in the Learning Commons and then organizes the various leadership teams to carry out those program elements. We recommend four partnership teams that have responsibility for the entire Learning Commons program, although each school would create its own leadership team configuration:

The Learning Commons Partnership Teams

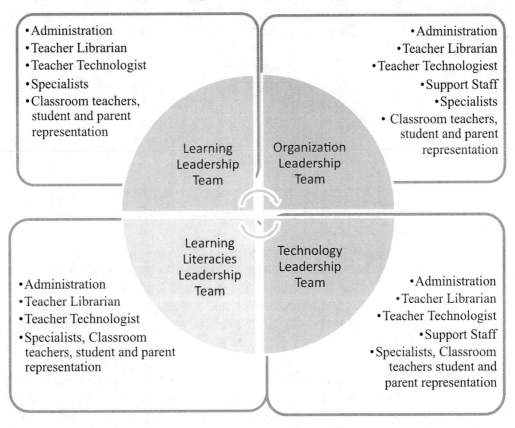

- Administration
- Teacher Librarian
- Teacher Technologist
- Specialists
- Classroom teachers, student and parent representation

- Administration
- Teacher Librarian
- Teacher Technologiest
- Support Staff
- Specialists
- Classroom teachers, student and parent representation

Learning Leadership Team

Organization Leadership Team

Learning Literacies Leadership Team

Technology Leadership Team

- Administration
- Teacher Librarian
- Teacher Technologist
- Specialists, Classroom teachers, student and parent representation

- Administration
- Teacher Librarian
- Teacher Technologist
- Support Staff
- Specialists, Classroom teachers student and parent representation

- **The Organization Leadership Team -** The lead teachers are a full-time teacher-librarian and a full-time teacher technologist who act as coordinators. As the professional staff of the Learning Commons, they apply their personal strengths and specialist training to the ignition of collaborative and experimental learning programs. These professionals understand and create a client side organization rather than a command and control operation. In addition, they have the time and administrative support to bring vital programming into fruition. They spend the majority of their time building, teaching, and assessing learning experiences and experimental programs as co-teachers with the classroom instructors. For example:

  o The Learning Commons teacher technologist concentrates on instructional computing rather than on administrative functions.

  o The teacher librarian concentrates on collaboration as opposed to focusing on the functioning of the Open Commons.

  o Specialists such as reading coaches, counselors, learning specialists, art, music, PE, or other specialists have scheduled time in the Learning Commons in order to make an impact across the school.

  o All the specialists function as a professional learning community under the direction of the administrator charged with instructional excellence.

  o As a group, these professionals plan, work, and assess their impact on teaching and learning.

  o Student representatives are included on all leadership teams (not just the Geeks or gifted students, but the average and struggling students have a voice).

- **The Technology Leadership Team–** The group of professionals, administrators and learners charged with leadership of technology, guide, vision, implement, budget for, and together create the technological environment of both the physical Learning Commons and its virtual counterpart.

- **The Learning Literacies Leadership Team–** This team focuses its efforts on the skill levels needed to propel each learner to success. Reading skills, information literacy, media literacy, and other emergent literacies are the province of their attention. Learning how to learn beyond minimal levels is seen as the mission of the entire faculty, albeit the specialization of various professionals.

- **Learning Leadership Team–** This team concentrates its efforts on building excellence in teaching and learning both in the Learning Commons and throughout the school. They worry about what learners know, are able to do and their deep understanding. They are particularly concerned with the range of professional development, the action research, the various learning initiatives of the entire school and the plan for sustainable school improvement.

- **Learning Commons Specialist Staff.** All specialists in the school including administration, subject specific specialists such art, music, or physical education; teacher technologists, teacher librarians, counselors, and even nurses constitute the specialist staff of the Learning Commons. One might consider these professionals as the PLC of experts who rise up from compartmental departments to influence the direction of the entire learning community. They drive the Experimental Learning Center of the Learning Commons whether officed there physically or virtually; for a part or a full day. These specialists are calendared to partner with classroom teachers. Learning activities are planned, taught, and assessed jointly with one or more of these specialists. As professionals, they have the opportunity to infuse and integrate their specialty into the school as a whole as well as in their own subject areas. Examples might include the following:

  - The school nurse may partner with the social studies teacher on a unit about drug abuse.

  - A teacher librarian integrates information literacy with various research projects.

  - The teacher technologist is assisting students in the creation of virtual field trips around their city or across the world.

  - The reading coach and the teacher librarian are conducting virtual book clubs that cross grade levels and school boundaries as they seek to increase the amount of reading and the love of reading.

  - The music teacher is infusing music across the curriculum in addition to directing a band, orchestra, or choir.

  - The counselor is pushing career studies into every subject or discipline in order to stimulate a vision of opportunities and how to prepare for them.

- **Administrative Leadership.** The administrator of the school charged with instructional improvement is a vital player in the planning and implementation of a vibrant and functioning Learning Commons for the school by providing leadership in person or virtually. This administrative leader understands the central role of an information-rich and technology-rich instructional environment and makes the Experimental Learning Center the focal point of school improvement.

- **Support Staff.** Support personnel include technicians, clerical assistants, and any other assistants who work in the Learning Commons or computer laboratory. These support persons take on the major responsibility of the "warehouse" under the direction of the teacher technologist and teacher librarian who are concentrating the bulk of their time on improving instruction. Support personnel may have credentials such as certificates in technology or have had short courses in the operation of the functions of the Open Commons. They keep networks up and running, collections circulating, handle the calendars of the Open Commons and the computer lab for scheduled classes and free flow of individuals, small groups, and full classes that do not require the services of the professionals. Besides training, these personnel are very organized, friendly, service-oriented, and problem solvers. They understand and are able to implement client-side policies established by the professionals in order to make the Learning Commons attractive to both students and teachers alike. Every Open Commons has the equivalent of a full-time support person in addition to the full-time teaching professionals. Larger schools will require multiple support personnel to keep the traffic of the center scheduled, productive, and satisfied.

Below, we highlight the roles and preparation of various specialists. All specialists have preparation as teachers first, adding their specialties on top. This prepares them not only to be good teachers in their own right, but to enhance learning across the learning community rather than teach in their specialty alone.

- **The Teacher Librarian** – All teacher librarians are master teachers in their own right and embrace co-teaching with others all across the school. Their knowledge of curriculum, instructional design, learning science, and leadership is enhanced by the discipline of library and information science where they add information theory, information systems, multimedia resources, collection building, and a host of other issues dealing with information in a high tech world. They are also comfortable learning any new technological system and software needed to be fluent alongside the best of their users. As information specialists they are valuable resources to learners and teachers; as specialist teachers they combine their expertise to provide needed instructional interventions and differentiated teaching and learning support. They are people persons who understand a client side organization as opposed to command and control that has been the structure of the past. They invest in supervision of the support staff of the Learning Commons but ensure that the majority of their time is devoted to teaching and learning rather than fine-tuning the warehouse of the Open Commons.

- **The Teacher Technologist** – Like the teacher librarian, teacher technologists are teachers first. Their principal education as an instructional designer and a great teacher in their own right trumps their concerns for equipment, networks, and software. They are visionaries as they match up the various available technologies to enhance learning; they are always looking for new applications that will boost achievement of the learners. As teachers, they model the use of technology as they co-teach with classroom teachers and partner with teacher librarians in the push toward excellence. They supervise the technical support staff who keeps the systems, networks, equipment and software funning and reliable 24/7. The majority of their day is spent co-teaching rather than fixing or troubleshooting problems. Their interactions with learners make not only the geeks approach them but also the mainstream learner and in particular, those who do not have access to technology in the home. They cry access, access, access as they teach learners to construct their own information spaces, personal learning networks, and bending social networking skills into their academic opportunities.

- **The Teacher Librarian/Teacher technologist** – In smaller schools, where there are not positions for both the teacher librarian and the teacher technologist, a teacher with both sets of expertise is selected. This may be a teacher technologist who has taken coursework in library and information science or a teacher librarian who has excellent instructional technology education. These professionals have the best backgrounds of both worlds as they focus their efforts on co-teaching with the faculty and building client-side organizational elements.

- **The Realities of the Learning Commons Staffing** – To merely declare the reinvention of the school library and computer laboratory does not make it so. For the past half century, schools have struggled to have both professionals and support staffing in the libraries and more recently in computer labs. State and provinces across North America provide uneven support for professionals and specialists depending on the view of essential staffing to make a school and learning community function. Financial exigencies in a district or board put pressures on administrators to target either the size of the specialist staff, the number of classroom teachers, or both. The view across the years gives us clues to what hasn't worked. The Lance and Todd[3] research is very clear when it comes to assessing impact of the library and the technology of the school. In both places, the lack of either professional or support personnel in these two centers negates much or most of their impact on teaching and learning. Support personnel alone do not have the expertise to make a difference in teaching and learning because they concentrate their attention on organizational or technical matters. Likewise, professionals without support personnel get tied to organizational systems that distract from their real work. The result has been little impact for dollars expended with the conclusion being that neither the library or computer labs earn their keep. It is as if the school was to buy a school bus without wheels and then wonder why kids are not getting to school.

---

[3] See the "Research and School Libraries" tab at http://www.davidvl.org

- **The Qualities of the Learning Commons Professionals** – Like all other organizations, success depends on the type of people pushing the vision of the organization. Well-meaning and visionary plans are either spoiled or implemented based on the day to day actions of both professionals and support personnel. Making a radical change from command and control to client side requires leadership, flexibility, risk taking, persistence, and hard work. Administrators are advised to select professionals with the qualities necessary to become learner centered and who will be catalysts for change. Rigidity founded in tradition has no place in the current changing world.

Systems and Networks that Support the Learning Commons Organization

- **On-Demand Networks** – The Learning Commons is the place to begin wireless networking for expected, future computing devices. It becomes the "Starbucks" access center of the school with this service extending out into the rest of the school as funding permits. The capacity of this instructional computing network is sufficient to handle the traffic and the volume of materials trying to be delivered. An example is the network capable of delivering two way audio and video. As learners create their own materials, the networks must be capable of handling these productions and storing them for further use.

- **On Demand User Friendly Support** – Every learner and teacher deserves prompt, friendly, and supportive assistance in order to realize the goal of transparent technology in the support of teaching and learning.

Scenarios

- **The Radical Shift.** When the leadership team of a school district, admittedly affluent, decided to implement one on one computing and equip every teacher with a plethora of technology, they realized that few of the current teaching staff had the expertise or the background to use what they were willing to provide. In a district-wide professional development session, the leadership team announced the radical change and also announced that every opportunity would be afforded the faculty to acquire the needed expertise over a two-year period. After the first year of immersion and facing the second year of major progress, the revolution was well under way, but some faculty, uncomfortable with the shift sought employment elsewhere. (Based on an actual interview with the superintendent by one of the authors).

- **A Teacher Librarian Makes the Shift.** Difficult financial times in one school district forced a teacher librarian to be half time in two different schools. In an interview with this teacher librarian two years after the change, she related the following story: At first she was heart-broken about not having the opportunity to be full time and in control of a single school library. A major positive was that each of the two buildings would have a full time support person there all day every day. The teacher librarian asked herself, "What is it that I do that makes the most impact on teaching and learning?" She decided that it was not the day to day operation of the facility, but the planning, co-teaching, and assessment of learning activities. Since the support personnel were quite competent, she turned over the calendars of the libraries to them. Then she created a second calendar for her clients. She announced to both faculties that she would be available to partner with them on learning experiences. Based on her reputation, the faculty at both schools began to sign up on her calendar. She created a flexible schedule so that sometimes, she was full time at one site and other weeks, full time at the other depending on the demands of the various learning experiences that were in progress. At first, there was limited demand for her time, but as the year progressed, more and more teachers and grade level teams were requesting her collaboration. By the end of the second year, she was concerned about her own burn out. But, in retrospect, she had learned that the administrivia, such a part of her former job, had not been missed; that the enormous satisfaction of watching and leading a push for teaching and learning excellence was paying huge dividends. She was looking forward to going back full time as teacher librarian in one of the schools, but with a whole new vision of what her new experience had taught her about priorities. (based on an actual interview)

- **When Coaches Discover a New Role.** In a large urban school district, a literacy coach and a newly appointed teacher librarian decided to pursue a masters in library and information science together. When they discovered in the instructional design course that they had to carry out an exemplary unit with a classroom teacher in their school or face failure in the class, they first discussed the possibilities. Both discovered that they had one thing in common: both of them were having difficulty getting into the classroom because teachers were saying that there was no time to do anything except prepare their students for the test. Selecting a prospective client, they invited the teacher to have lunch with them. They pleaded their case. Feeling sorry for her colleagues facing this obligatory "assignment," the teacher agreed. The resulting unit was so successful that the team reported: "We felt as if the joy of teaching was back in education!" (based on a log of the assignment to the professor. P.S. They got an A.)

- **Getting Started.** The teacher technologist and the teacher librarian met to discuss ways they could integrate their agendas better into the school so that teaching and learning would be affected. Feeling that a shift to a Learning Commons concept might be too radical, they proposed a first step to the principal; that professional development be conducted in the library. They cleared a space for larger groups and arranged for a conference room. Access to technology in these spaces was exemplary and there was easy access to the print resources. The two specialists arranged their own calendars so they would be available for as many sessions as possible. They began to experience increased acceptance of their professional ideas for the integration of technology and print. In March of the school year, they proposed to the principal that the official organization of the Experimental Learning Center take place. A summer action research workshop later, they were under way. After the staff had the action research PD everyone was ready to open the Experimental Learning Commons and test all school initiatives here.

- **Living Textbooks.** The skyrocketing price of textbooks for every discipline, for every learner, was the tipping point for change in a large secondary school. Administration demanded a more cost efficient method of information delivery. A committee of specialist, classroom teachers and students was immediately charged with the problem. During an early brainstorming session a teacher remarked to the group how much he appreciated the Pathfinders the teacher librarian prepared for his units this term. Others piped up with similar comments. A student on the committee demonstrated how she used I Google pages to keep up-to-date. Then the big Aha! Subject teams and students are now busy working with Learning Commons specialists to prepare Pathfinders with RRS feeds of up-to-the-minute, subject specific data which they plan to feed into student I Google pages. Administrators were happy with the savings and agreed to allocate much of the textbook budget to purchasing needed databases and e-books.

Over to You. Discuss with Us at:http//schoollearningcommons.pbwiki.com

- What organizational features do you already have that lead the way toward the client side structure?

- Will this new structure save the school money?

- How will we measure effectiveness of the new Learning Commons?

Resources

Professional Documents:

- Marzano, Robert J., Timothy Waters, and Brian A. McNulty. *School Leadership That Works: From Research to Results*. ASCD, 2005.

- Marzano, Robert J. *What Works in Schools: Translating Research into Action*. ASCD, 2003

- Whitaker, Todd. *What Great Principals Do Differently: Fifteen Things That Matter Most*. Eye on Education, 2002.

- Waters, Tom and Greg Cameron. *The Balanced Framework: Connecting Vision with Action*. McRel. 2007.

- Wiggins, Grant and Jay McTighe. *Schooling by Design: Mission, Action, and Achievement*. ASCD, 2007.

- Carr, JoAnn, ed. *Leadership for Excellence: Insights of National Cchool Library Media Program of the Year Awardd Winners*. AASL, 2008.

- Wiggins, Grant and Jay McTighe. *Scjhooling by Design: Mission, Action, and Achievement*. ASCD, 2007.

- Tomlinson, Carol Ann, Kay Brimijohn, and Lane Narvaez. *The Differentiated School: Making Revolutionary Changes in Teaching and Learning*. ASCD, 2008.

Professional Organizations

- While the usual educational organizations, particularly those for administrators have some emphasis on leadership and management, we recommend that an eye toward business management organizations may be of some assistance when looking to how client side structures work and flourish.

Evidence Based Practice
and the Learning Commons

Evidence Based Practice is a fairly new approach to school improvement that has its roots in the fields of medicine and health care. It is interesting to note the parallels between education, medicine, and health care; the major one being making a difference to the well being of the client.

The chemistry that makes a difference in the Library Commons is distilled from Evidence-Based Practice (EBP) being applied to improving teaching and learning. Teachers and learners as well, make informed decisions about improving their performance by considering 'best practice' theories, research or 'what the experts say', as well as careful assessment of their own experiences.

In an Evidence-Based Practice approach, for every experience in the Learning Commons clients ask themselves, what worked, what didn't, and why. They continue to use their experiences to improve performance and to advocate for needed resources, staffing, and changes in systems. The guesswork is then removed from teaching and learning because decisions related to both are made based on results.

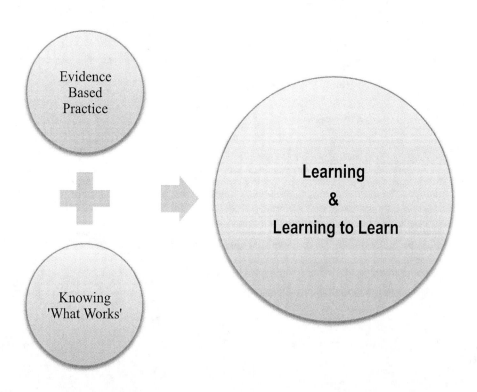

Ross Todd[1] outlines three core beliefs that are critical to the success of applying EBP in the Learning Commons:

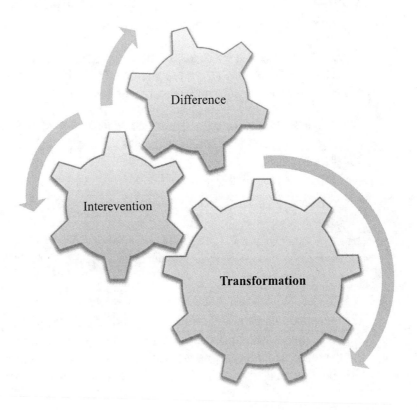

Difference: the provision of information and information services makes a difference to the lives of people. This means that conducting a learning experience in the midst of an information-rich and technology-rich environment has more potential of making a difference than the same learning experience done in the information-poor environment of the classroom where resources consist of the textbook and lecture.

Intervention: The key role of the teacher-librarian (and other specialists) centers on pedagogical intervention that directly impacts on, and shapes the quality of student learning through their engagement with information. This means that two heads are better than one. At every opportunity, the classroom teacher co-teaches with one or more specialists in the school.

Transformation: The role of pedagogical intervention is to bring on transformation. Learning takes place, and the lives of our students are transformed. The knowledge, skills, attitudes and values of learners are shaped and grow through their engagement in the school Learning Commons and its pedagogical interventions. This means that the

---

[1] Loertscher, David V. and Ross J. Todd *We Boost Achievement.* Hi Willow Research & Publishing, 2006.

instructional units and learning activities of the Learning Commons should showcase the very best teaching and learning of the entire school.

Are these three principles happening in the Learning Commons? How do we know? What is being documented? What evidence do we have that the impact of the Learning Commons activities are spiraling out from this hub into the school as a whole? Is there any evidence that the Learning Commons is transforming the entire school into a healthier environment where improvement is sustained?

Certainly, the idea that one measurement, a single test or small set of tests would be able to accurately assess all that we are interested in building is fool hardy. It is not just a single reading and/or math score that indicates the health of the school or its results.

We look, instead, at a variety of evidence as indicators of continuous coordinated progress. Evidence based practice launches schools on a continuum towards sustainable excellence.

We recommend a variety of measures including triangulation of evidence as a barometer of health. In this system, a variety of simple-to-collect and analyze data are being collected at the organizational level, the teaching unit level, and the learner level. Examined together they point to the direction for progress toward excellence.

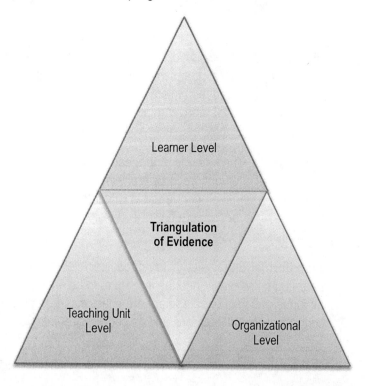

There are many measures that could be taken; a selection of those that work best is in order. The following lists are a few of the possibilities.

The Challenge: To use measures from all levels to triangulate the view of impact.

Learner Level	Teaching Unit Level	Organizational Level
• Completed organizers • Rubrics • Reflection/learning logs • Self/peer evaluation • Research folders • Source sheets • Checklists • Evidence of goal setting • Student conferencing notes • Video tape of students working or sharing • Photos of students working • Test results and reporting comments	• Collaboration logs • Records of debriefing of lessons/units • Copies of lessons and units • Documentation of skills taught over time • Workshops designed to help teach and integrate information literacy and other skills • Imporved teacher confidence integrating technologies • Increased requests for resources, lessons, professional development and other services • Repeat collaboration	• Circulation statistics • Collection mapping • Quality of collection (inclusive, curriculum support, print and electronic, variety, interests) • Budget reports • Student and teacher comments • Access to physical and virtual collection for all • Access to computers and other technologies • Before and after video or photos • Engaged, eager, students and teachers

Empowering the Learner

Benefits of EBP to learners, in the Learning Commons, are twofold. To begin with students receive first class instruction and support because teachers are engaged in making adjustments and changes to their teaching methodology based on real evidence. Secondly students gain from their own reflective approach to making decisions about how they can best participate and learn to receive optimum results. Metacognition is embedded in the EBP process. Once they begin to take responsibility for their learning, students analyze what they do and how it works for them and they make decisions informed by evidence/results. Students realize that the Learning Commons programs are designed to provide them with the skills and tools to help them excel. As students apply EBP they are learning how to learn. In the chart below, we list some of the indicators that learners are consciously applying EBP to their own growth. Look to AASL[2] for dispositions that every learner should acquire to be successful.

Doing

- Designing graphic organizers
- Testing ideas with others
- Experimenting with presentation techniques
- Trying out new software and hardware
- Trying different note making strategies
- Keeping a learning portfolio
- Recording reflections on learning

Learning to Learn

- Responsibility and ownership of learning
- Reflection
- Collaborative knowledge building
- Problem solving
- Decision making
- Critical thinking
- Risk taking
- Constructivist learning

Knowing and Understanding

- Metacognition of learning process
- Determing personal strengths
- Setting goals and planning for improvement
- Applying knowledge of brain based learning
- Transfer learning to new or different situations
- Making informed decisions about strategies and technologies to use
- Taking action based on personal research, discoveries, and conclusions

How are these qualities measured? In a client-side organization, the learners shoulder the responsibility for self-assessment rather than assuming that adult evaluators will do it for them. Learners' attitudes thus move from assuming victimization to taking control of their learning success. The role of the professionals is to facilitate and coach learners about how to gather and analyze evidence of their own growth as the work in the Learning Commons. The following diagram illustrates the desired growth mindset.

---

[2] *AASL Standards for the 21st Century Learner.* At:
http://www.acrl.org/ala/aasl/aaslproftools/learningstandards/standards.cfm

I can demonstrate what I know, can do, and deeply understand [3] to myself and others by:

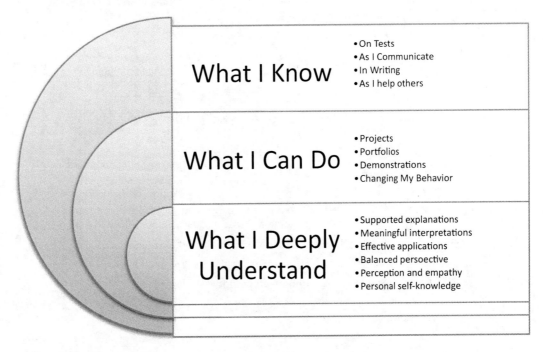

What I Know	• On Tests • As I Communicate • In Writing • As I help others
What I Can Do	• Projects • Portfolios • Demonstrations • Changing My Behavior
What I Deeply Understand	• Supported explanations • Meaningful interpretations • Effective applications • Balanced persoective • Perception and empathy • Personal self-knowledge

I can demonstrate that I am learning how to learn by:

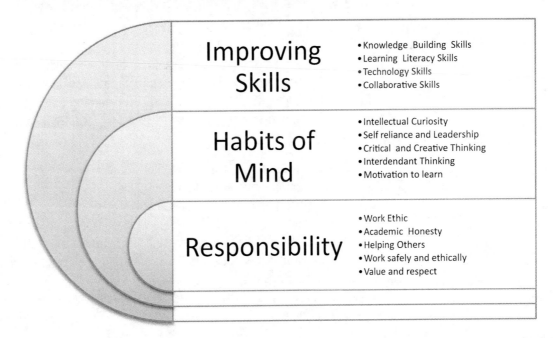

Improving Skills	• Knowledge Building Skills • Learning Literacy Skills • Technology Skills • Collaborative Skills
Habits of Mind	• Intellectual Curiosity • Self reliance and Leadership • Critical and Creative Thinking • Interdendant Thinking • Motivation to learn
Responsibility	• Work Ethic • Academic Honesty • Helping Others • Work safely and ethically • Value and respect

---

[3] Adapted from Wiggins, Grant and Jay McTighe, *Understanding By Design 2nd edition.* ASDC, 2005. P 82-104

The professionals will assist learners to develop strategies for gathering evidence to demonstrate their learning. They will show students how to use these measures to set goals for improvement.

Sample Measures for Learners:

- Analyzing my performance on formative and summative tests.
- Tracking the amount read for pleasure and for topics I am studying.
- Logging a journey through a research assignment.
- Defending the quality of information I used for my report/paper/project.
- Self-assessing of products and projects I create.
- Logging my contributions to groups, the classroom, and the school.
- Giving feedback to teachers and specialists about learning units connected to the Learning Commons.
- Rating my progress in taking command of my own learning. Am I on the path to excellence?

Empowering the Teacher

Teachers have the support of the teacher-librarian and other specialists in the Learning Commons to help them determine what evidence to gather, how to analyze the data, and then how to apply the findings to improve teaching and learning. Becoming a reflective practitioner is a process of discovery. Several methods of EBP are suggested for maximum results:

- **At the Learner Level**
  - Normal formative and summative tests
  - Monitoring learner self-assessment
  - Consider the percent of learners who meet, exceed, and struggle with expectations for collaborative units with specialists in the Learning Commons. How does this percent compare with expectations when teaching alone?
  - The results for learners of action research projects in the Experimental Learning Center.

- **At the Teaching Unit Level**
  - Analysis of journals/notes/teaching plans kept for collaborative units and action research studies. Are two heads better than one?

- o Analysis of the characteristics of learners who benefit the most and least from learning units co-taught in the Learning Commons.
- o Identifying strategies that have positive results.

- **At the Organization Level**
  - o The number/quality of collaborative and action research projects of individual, grade level, department level and the entire faculty
  - o Access to technology and rotating materials in the classrooms during the day.
  - o Access to technology and materials extending 24/7/365.
  - o Access to specialists, Learning Commons availability, and Experimental Learning Center availability.

When data are flowing into the various leadership teams of the school from learners, teachers and specialists, a number of benefits accrue to the teachers, the leadership teams, and the conversations of various professional learning communities. We list a few of these below. Individual teachers will have other items to add from their personal experiences so we encourage you to make your own lists.

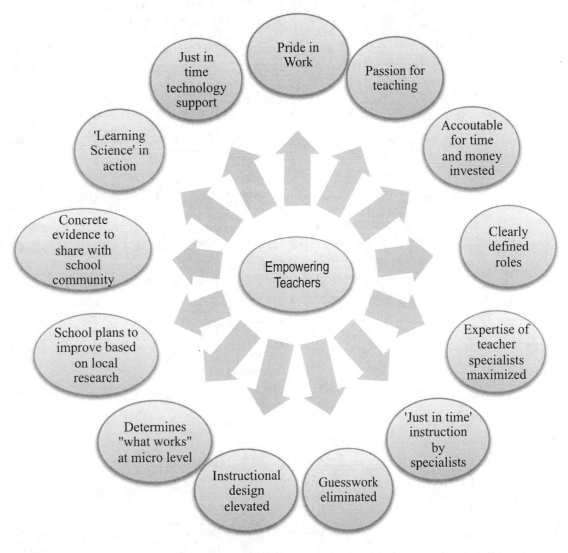

Empowering the Specialists

All of the specialists in the school take a reflective approach to their contributions to teaching and learning. When they are co-teaching in the Learning Commons and the Experimental Learning Center they are constantly testing the notion that two heads are better than one, but they are also interested in the impact of integrating their own curriculum responsibilities and best practice specialties into learning units. For example, the teacher librarian is testing the idea that integrated information literacy instruction is more effective when integrated into learning activities as just in time intervention rather than taught separately. Likewise, learning to work in a wiki environment is better integrated into a real learning experience rather than a contrived one since it needs authenticity to engage learners.

5 Key Things Specialists Do Every Day to Make a Difference:

- Collaborate with teachers to build, co-teach, and assess solid and engaging learning experiences.

- Analyze the data from learner assessments to keep improving collaborative efforts. Ask are we pushing every learner toward excellence?

- Teach integrated skills that match their specialty, e.g. information literacy (teacher librarians), Target specific reading skills as learners are doing research (reading coaches).

- Motivate learners to read more (yes, this is every specialist's responsibility).

- Work with the leadership teams on continuous school improvement.

The Learning Commons as Evidence Based Practice Central

By triangulating or taking into account data from various sources, the school leadership teams and professional learning communities make decisions and adjust policies based on evidence rather than whim or well-meaning dictates. It is all a part of learning that works in our school with our students, with our parents, and in our community in the advance towards sustainable excellence.

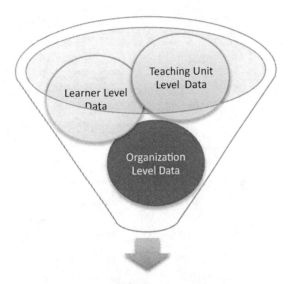

Decisions and Policy Changes

Several methods of EBP are suggested for maximum results:

1) *Ongoing assessment and evaluation of students using diagnostic, formative, and summative tools as well as standardized test results.*

2) *Teacher journaling of critical moments in their personal learning journeys.*

3) *Professional portfolios built over time to track teacher growth and goals.*

4) *Systematic tracking and documentation of Learning Commons.*

5) *Regular action research projects to explore questions and test out possibilities.*

6) *Collaborative analysis of evidence.*

Action Research as the Focus of the Experimental Learning Commons

Action research is different from scientific research in one major way. Action research happens in the real world where variables cannot be controlled, as one would do in a laboratory experiment. Action research happens in real classrooms with real learners, or in this case in an actual Experimental Learning Center. It takes the best theories of education and research results and applies them to a local situation. As they embark on Action Research practitioners ask themselves questions such as; Does this idea work in my inner-city school? Does this strategy work in a school where ten different languages are spoken? How can I differentiate strategies for my special needs students?

The steps of action research are well known:

- Begin with a research question.
- Decide on a methodology/strategy to test the question.
- Conduct the research/collect the data.
- Analyze the data.
- Draw conclusions.
- Ask: So what?
- Report the results
- What's next?

Senese reminds us that our emphasis is on "how to" teach and "why" teach, not "what" to teach.[4] Examples of action research projects that would be appropriate for the Experimental Learning Commons follow:

- **Impact of Background Knowledge.** Marzano's research[5] encourages teachers to build background knowledge as a prelude to the main event of any topical study. Consider the following scenario. In our school, we have a variety of languages spoken so we decide to test the idea of spending a bit more time on background building, using a variety of media to see if it makes a difference in the main part of a topical unit. Together, the classroom teacher and the teacher librarian select and allow learners to be exposed to Internet sites, books on the topic, video, pictures, podcasts in various languages – anything that we can find that would introduce a topic to learners ranging from novice to experts who have different language and cultural backgrounds. We decide to spend three class periods in the Experimental Learning Commons with the class as they "consume" the materials we have found and ask them in small groups to create graphic organizers about what they are reading, viewing, and hearing. The class then builds the questions together for the main event of the learning unit and we continue on as we normally would. We assess the learners along the way and at the end. As a team, we look at the results together. What type of learner seems to have met and exceeded expectations? If there is another class in the school that studied the same topic but did not spend the time on background building, how do the two groups compare? How did these experiences affect student knowledge of topic related vocabulary? Did the learners seem to be better prepared for the main event? Why? What media and resources seemed to work the best? Why? What did the learners think about this technique to help them master the content better? What would we change the next time? As we present our results to our professional learning community, were we and they ready to make similar trials in other classrooms and other topics?

- **Eliminating the Cut, Paste and Plagiarism Behavior of Learners.** Loertscher, Koechlin and Zwaan[6] postulate that when learners have the habit of just cutting and pasting information from the Internet or other sources and turning it in as their own work, there is a simple solution: change the assignment so that cutting and pasting doesn't work. Instead, learners have to consume the information, think about it, analyze it, and work with others to massage it, or use it in some way in order to fulfill the assignment. Design the assignment so that analysis and synthesis is mandatory.

---

[4] See a similar list by Joseph C. Senese, "What Are the Conditions That Sustain Teacher Research?" at: What are the Conditions that Sustain Teacher Research? At: http://educ.queensu.ca/~ar/aera2000/senese.pdf

[5] Marzano, Robert J. *Classroom Instruction That Works*. ASCD, 2004.

[6] Loertscher, David V., Carol Koechlin, and Sandi Zwaan. *Beyond Bird Units: 18 Models for Teaching in Information-Rich and Technology-Rich Environments*. Hi Willow Research & Publishing, 2007.

Consider the following scenario. The teacher librarian and one language arts teacher volunteer to demonstrate this technique to the rest of the faculty in the Experimental Learning Center and invite visitors at any time during the demonstration and promise to report their project to the faculty as a whole. Learners are doing reports on famous African Americans. In a Google Spreadsheet, they research and post various facts from authoritative information sources about the person's childhood, education, problems faced, challenges faced, defeats, victories, achievements, and tributes paid them from others. Each cell in the spreadsheet contains a sentence or two pulled from the original source together with the citation for that information. When the spreadsheet has been loaded, the class jigsaws and groups analyze (look for connections, trends, similarities, differences, cause and effect...) each of the categories across people and enter their conclusions in a final right-hand column. After this analysis has been completed, new groups do an analysis of all the characteristics across people; decide on similarities and differences; and, draw conclusions. Each group then meets with an invited African American Guest to present their findings and discuss "how they overcame." Finally, each leaner writes a personal response about the research journey and the conclusions drawn about people who overcome any obstacle. The teacher librarian and the classroom teacher reported the major difference made in the learning to the faculty as a whole. Five other classroom teachers volunteered to try similar action research projects and report back to test whether this type of strategy would be worth full-scale implementation in the school.

The success of such action research projects and the invitation to other teachers to observe the research in the fishbowl of the Experimental Learning Commons requires certain collaborative behaviors on the part of the professionals:

- An openness to collaboration and co-teaching
- The gift of time to accomplish the research
- An emphasis on helping every learner achieve excellence
- Recognition by administrators and peers for honesty and risk-taking[7]

Other brief examples of projects and research done to inform the professional learning community might include:

- The teacher-librarian tracks all collaborations and Learning Commons interventions to determine teachers and classes to target for future work.

- The teacher technologist and the teacher librarian help students develop systems to monitor use and effectiveness of popular search tools during a collaborative unit

---

[7] See a similar list by Joseph C. Senese, "What Are the Conditions That Sustain Teacher Research?" at: What are the Conditions that Sustain Teacher Research? At: http://educ.queensu.ca/~ar/aera2000/senese.pdf

with a classroom teacher. Adaptations or enhancements are designed to meet the needs of specific students.

- Teachers and specialists compare results of special needs students when using a variety of differentiation and 'just in time' intervention strategies.

- Learners, specialists, and a classroom teacher experiment with a new rubric, for self-assessment, that has been proposed to go school-wide.

One note of caution about action research: The research results findings of work done with one classroom apply to that classroom only. However, as the same technique is used over and over in the school, patterns will begin to emerge so that the leadership team can make policy with confidence. As we all realize, situations can change and subsequently negate what we know. For example, a school's demographics can change rather rapidly so that strategies and teaching techniques that were successful previously, no longer work as well. Thus they need to focus on the current needs of the learner. Professional learning communities always keep this idea in mind as they focus on sustainable, evolutionary, excellence.

The Learning Partnership Teams

All the leadership teams, classroom teachers, and learners are engaged in the collection, analysis and interpretation of EBPdata to inform the school improvement plan.

Systems and Networks that Support Evidence Based Practice

To be successful in the pursuit of excellence with a foundation of research and best practice, the entire tone and culture of the school must be pointed in that direction. What works? What research and best practice is out there and being published that we should examine and try? We are well aware of the various cycles of education. Old ideas once in favor seem to come around again with new names and fanfare. New strategies are often dictated without local experimentation or action research. **This may be one of the best arguments for a Learning Commons with a vibrant Experimental Learning Center program.** When the entire faculty realizes that administrators are serious about sustainable school improvement many barriers fall. Experimentation and risk taking are encouraged and rewarded.

Scenarios

- **Fishbowl Findings.** As co-teaching units between specialists and classroom teachers began in the school, the specialists were assigned the task of documenting on a large chart the units they co-taught for each month. During the professional development community meeting each month, the principal would select one of the previous month's units at random. Those involved would give an impromptu five minute report highlighting the percent of learners who met or exceeded unit expectations. The challenges of learners who did not succeed were explained and ideas from the entire faculty were sought for improvement. The principal "salted the audience" the first few times to guarantee that the discussion would be active, humorous, and productive. After that, the faculty settled into an informative and anticipated part of the learning community's meeting. Over time, the conversations became more and more complex and analytical, leading to some questions being developed for action research.

- **Real Time is Key.** A teacher librarian in a multicultural school was distressed with the lack of communication in Book Chat, her very well attended lunch club. Students seemed to like being part of the club but were reluctant to share, verbally. Suspecting this problem was related to language skills the teacher librarian met with ESL teachers, consulted with other teacher librarians, did some research on the Web2 environment and decided to try a wiki to extend the book club experience. Students were excited but slow to start, however after a few weeks the questions and comments started to flow. Once students had gained confidence discussing the novels she partnered with two other school districts involved in the same book club program to set up video conferencing sessions. Each week students took turns introducing the novel for discussion. An author was invited to join one of the video conferencing sessions and the enthusiasm was infectious. The teacher librarian summed it up nicely in a media release to her school district. "Our students come from such a wide range of cultural backgrounds, and to see them come together as a community on the wiki and then take that step further and watch them find the courage to build new connections with students from other communities has been an enriching experience for all of us." The teacher librarian reviewed the wiki history and archived video to document student growth, and has plans to share this evidence with her staff.

Over to You. Discuss with Us at: http//schoollearningcommons.pbwiki.com
- What steps could be taken to ease into an evidence-based practice organization?
- How can we take a critical incident and apply action research?

Resources

Foundational Ideas

- Sawyer, R. Keith, ed. *The Cambridge Handbook of the Learning Sciences.* Cambridge University Press, 2005.

- Popham, W. James. *TransFormative Assessment. ASCD, 2008.*

Professional Resources:

- Carol-Bruce, Cathy. *Creating Equitable Classrooms Through Action Research.* Corwin Press, 2007.

- Chaplin, Connie, David V. Loertscher, and Nancy A.S. Miller. *Sharing the Evidence: School Library Assessment Tools and Resources. 2nd ed.* Hi Willow Research & Publishing, 2008.

- Clauset, Karl H. *Schoolwide Action Research for Professional Learning Communities: Improving Student Learning Through the Whole Faculty.* Corwin Press, 2008.

- Costa, Arthur L. *The School as a Home for the Mind.* Corwin Press, 2008.

- Farmer, Lesley. *How to Conduct Action Research: A Guide for Library Media Specialists.* AASL, 2002.

- Habits of Mind http://www.habits-of-mind.net/

- Kelly, M.G. (Peggy) and Jon Haber. *Resources for Student Assessment.* ISTE, 2006.

- Koechlin, Carol and Sandi Zwaan. *Build Your Own Information Literate School.* Hi Willow Research & Publishing, 2006.

- Loertscher, David V. and Ross Todd. *We Boost Achievement.* Hi Willow Research & Publishing, 2006.

- Reeves, Douglas B. *Reframing Teacher Leadership to Improve Your School.* ASCD, 2008.

- Clauset, Karl H., Dale W. Lick, and Charlene U. Murphy. *Schoolwide Action Research for Professional Learning Communities.* Corwin Press, 2008.

Other Resources

- OSLA Toolkit http://www.accessola.com/osla/toolkit/intro.html

- Project Achievement http://www.davidvl.org/achieve.html

- Building Evidence Based Evidence through Action Research
http://www2.hawaii.edu/~vharada/vi-Building%20Evidence-12-03-jav.htm

- Action Research in the Grand Erie District School Board
  http://www.actionresearch.ca/

Professional Organizations:

- CARET Centre for Applied Research in Educational Technology
  http://caret.iste.org/index.cfm?fuseaction=resources

- IES Institute of Educational Sciences http://ies.ed.gov/ncee/wwc/
- American Educational Research Association http://www.aera.net/

- International Association of Learning Sciences http://www.isls.org/index.html

Connections with People and Ideas
and the Learning Commons

In this chapter, we identify major people and ideas across education that we believe advance the field toward excellence. Then, we make connections between those people and their ideas to propel libraries and computer labs into the very center of school improvement.

The Power of Action Research

Douglas B. Reeves, founder of the Leadership and Learning Center, in his book, *Reframing Teacher Leadership to Improve Your School* (ASCD; 2008), places action research at the center of school improvement. He posits that teachers become leaders when they are testing ideas from research in their classrooms and reporting the results on data walls or science-fair type expositions. The key to school improvement, then, is using evidence that our practices are effective based on increased learning. This follows the ideas of Reeves in his previous book *The Learning Leader* (ASCD, 2006) where he categorized the successful teacher is one who succeeds and knows why.

Learning Commons Connections: In the context of the Learning Commons we recommend that the Experimental Learning Center be the center of such research activity that informs the faculty as a whole. There is an atmosphere of collaboration in the achievement of excellence because everyone expects that this is a place in the school where experimentation is the central focus. It follows that a positive attitude toward continuous school improvement is likely to develop and be sustained across years and across faculty turnover or student demographic evolution. If the action research combines both the classroom teacher and one or more specialists such as the teacher librarian, then the focus of school improvement realizes impact of collaboration among the faculty. Such a focus would go a long way in promoting the idea that everyone has a stake in school improvement rather than just isolated teachers in closed classrooms. For example, the theme of the school year through its action research could be on the impact of actual collaborative teaching and learning resulting in a data wall exhibition for the school board, parent groups, the news media, presentations at professional conventions, and to any other interested audience. What is learned as a group becomes part of the repertoire of teaching strategies for the school.

Instructional Strategies

In: Robert J. Marzano, Debra J. Pickering, and Jane E. Pollock. *Classroom Instruction That Works: Research-Based Strategies for Increasing Student Achievement.* ASCD, 2001, the authors of this very popular book list nine strategies supported by research that are worth replicating in the classroom. They are:

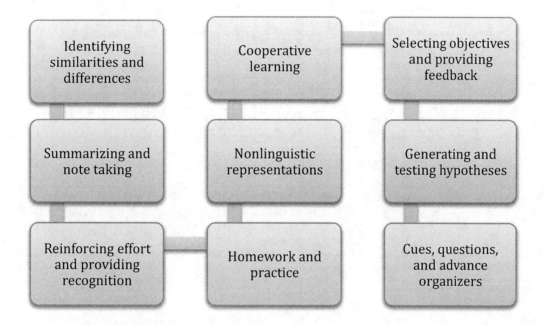

Learning Commons Connections: One of the benefits of the movement to base teaching and learning on more scientific principles has been collections of strategies like those above that are supported by research. These and other strategies form the foundational base of all teachers as they mature in their profession. However, teachers need to tailor, test, and reinvent these strategies as generations of learners and cultural backgrounds shift. Using the Experimental Learning Center to bring such conversations to the forefront as a collaborative rather than competitive focus seems to us to be a major step in the direction of school improvement.

Michael Fullan, Peter Hill, and Carmel Crevola

In their book: *Breakthrough* (Corwin Press, 2006), this trio proposes that to make major changes in education and make them sustainable, three components must form the core of instruction in the school:

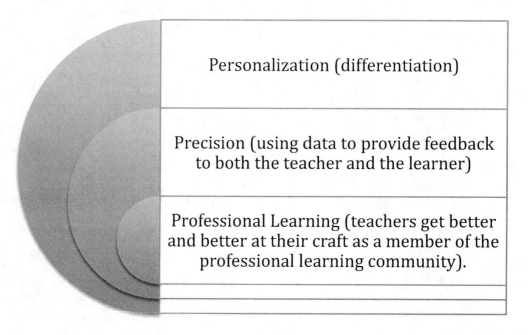

Personalization (differentiation)

Precision (using data to provide feedback to both the teacher and the learner)

Professional Learning (teachers get better and better at their craft as a member of the professional learning community).

They see a systematic effort that is not just discussed, but practiced and applied to the actual learning activities of the classroom.

Learning Commons Connections: It is not enough to have a professional development session and then assume that something will automatically change actual classroom practice. When the specialists of the school collaborate with the teachers to co-teach units of instruction, everyone in the building knows that new ideas are being tested in the Experimental Learning Community where all can observe and where teaching and learning is examined for excellence and better and better ideas are recommended and tested. It is then that the specialists follow such ideas out into the school as a whole complete with a feedback system for everyone. Each initiative is tracked and displayed in the Learning Commons providing a timeline of progress. Thus, diffusion of the initiative, strategy, policy, or operation is tracked on large graphic organizer charts for all to see and discuss. Sustainable school improvement becomes a part of striving for excellence – both in terms of the percent of students who achieved beyond expectations and teachers who keep improving.

Bernie Dodge and WebQuests

Bernie Dodge is well known for the inquiry projects that challenge users to complete a quest using Internet resources. Learners are grouped and face some type of problem. Each learner takes a different role as the group tackles the web-related task resulting in an authentic project or presentation. Recently, the thousands of WebQuests available have been compiled into a taxonomy to illustrate the types of tasks that have been developed around this model:

Taxonomy of WebQuest Tasks[1]

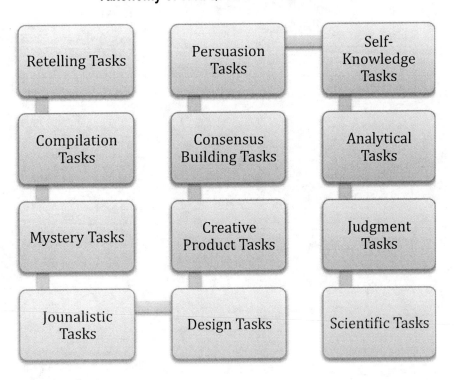

Learning Commons Connections: The various tasks of WebQuests compare in many ways to the think models created by Loertscher, Koechlin and Zwaan and presented in the Knowledge Building chapter of this book. Some of the best characteristics about WebQuests are their focus on engaging tasks, learner collaboration, and collaborative product building. At the conclusion of such learning activities, it is wise to build a culminating "big think" activity where the various teams of learners develop big ideas across the topics studied and also reflect on the journey they had in getting to their destination.

---

[1] For an explanation of each of the tasks, consult Bernie Dodge's website at: http://webquest.sdsu.edu/taskonomy.html

Backwards Design and the Six Facets of Learning:
Grant Wiggins and Jay McTighe

Wiggins and McTighe[2] have made an incredible contribution to teaching and learning through their development and popularization of using backwards design to help learners know, do, and deeply understand.

Steps in Backwards Design:

| Identify Desired Results | ➡ | Determine Acceptable Evidence | ➡ | Plan Learning Experiences and Instruction |

The Six Facets of Understanding

Explain	• Provide thorough and justifiable accounts of phenomena, facts, and data.
Interpret	• Tell meaningful stories, offer apt translations, provide a revealing historical or personal dimension to ideas and events; make subjects personal or accessible through images, anecdotes, analogies, and models.
Apply	• Effectively use and adapt what they know in diverse contexts.
Have Perspective	• See and hear points of view through critical eyes and ears; see the big picture.
Empathize	• Find value in what others might find odd, alien, or implausible; perceive sensitively on the basis of prior indirect experience.
Have Self Knowledge	• Perceive the personal style, prejudices, projections, and habits of mind that both shape and impede our own understanding; they are aware of what they do not understand and why understanding is so hard.

Learning Commons Connections: These elements are the foundational ideas of teaching and learning in the Learning Commons and a part of the major ideas being developed and tested in the Experimental Learning Center.

---

[2] Wiggins, Grant and Jay McTighe. *Understanding by Design.* Expanded 2nd ed. Prentice Hall, 2005.

Alan November

In his most reacent book: *Web Literacy for Educators* (Corwin Press, 2008).[3] November is concerned about the quality of information that ends up in student projects. He provides number suggestions to helping learners ascertain who is saying what to them for what reasons, for what gain, and when it was said. Teachers are encouraged to teach a variety of evaluative strategies such as investigating who created the website or looking at the extension such as .org, .edu, .com, or .gov. November rejects the notion that we should forbid the use of the Internet just because there is poor information, propaganda, even misleading information. Rather, we teach the learner to:

Harvest the Best

Leave the Rest

Learning Commons Connections: Since the rise of the Google search engine, the virus of cut and paste mentality has struck across the world. Teacher librarians, as one of the specialists in the schools have been waging a battle to help learners judge information quality before they embrace it as exactly what they need. In the Open Commons and the Experimental Learning Center, quality information is a foundational expectation whether the ideas come from the Internet, a book, a database, a newspaper, or an interview. Discernment of quality is a constant and not likely to be less important any time soon.

---

[3] See also Alan November's web page at: http://novemberlearning.com/

Critical Thinking

The Center for Critical Thinking[4] in Sonoma, California is one of a network of centers for critical thinking and publishes a variety of miniature guides to various aspects of critical thinking for use by learners and teachers. One of their excellent models appears as:

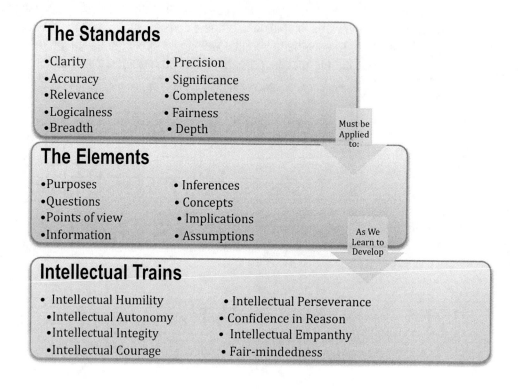

Learning Commons Connections: Critical thinking is a basic element built into learning activities that happen both in the Open Commons and the Experimental Learning Center. These skills are part of the information literacy skills taught by teacher librarians, part of any excursion on the Internet, part of the normal strategy of the classroom teacher. Like other literacies, critical thinking is best integrated into a topical exploration rather than taught as a topic in and of itself. When specialists and classroom teachers build learning activities, critical thinking should be on their checklist for integration planning.

---

[4] The Critical Thinking Community page at: http://www.criticalthinking.org/index.cfm

Stephen Krashen

Stephen Krashen backs up the idea with 100 years of research that kids who read widely score high; but, they also develop a number of characteristics that push them toward excellence.

The Reading Hypothesis[5]

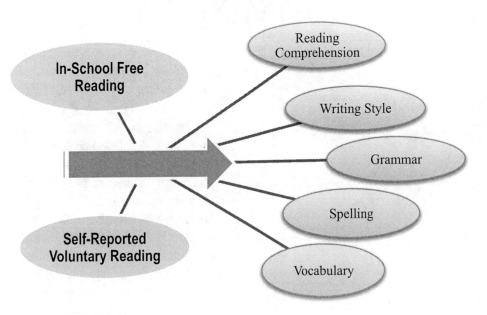

Learning Commons Connections: There is no stronger idea and support for the reinvention of the library into a Learning Commons than Krashen's hypothesis. It is here that learners and teachers have a plethora of materials they **want to read** and access to these materials is far beyond the norm of the past. Now with so much reading being done on the Internet and the very best fiction and nonfiction books available in the Learning Commons, there is really no excuse not to embrace the Krashen idea. Reading is not just skills. It is a life-long embracement. Teacher librarians should survey the learners to find out whether they like to read. With any percentage under 100% yes, then a revolution in the reading program needs to be considered.

---

[5] Krashen, Stephen. *The Power of Reading.* 2nd ed. Libraries Unlimited, 2006, p. 17.

David Warlick

David Warlick has a very popular blog: 2 cents Worth at: http://davidwarlick.com/2cents/ His musings on technology, the people and conferences he attends help the reader keep up with the current happenings in the field. In one of his columns, he describes his own personal learning network – a neighborhood of sorts that connects him to the world.

David Warlick's Personal Learning Network[6]

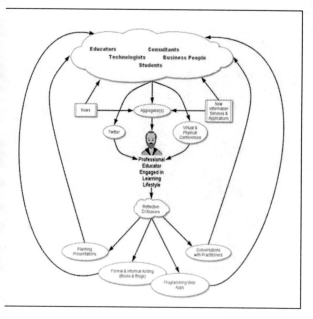

I see my PLN as having three basic components.

1. **The Network** — People who have things to say that help me do my job, and dynamic information sources that provide me with the raw materials I need.
2. **The Tools** — Essentially, the avenues of communication through which I connect with people and information sources — conduits that often add value to the information.
3. **My Own Personal Echo Chamber** — This is my own world view from which I teach, where ideas from my PLN bounce around off the walls of my mind and off of other ideas, either losing momentum and fading away, or generating energy and growing.

Learning Commons Connections: We advocate that all young people learn how to command their own information space and learn to govern themselves within this space. Whether through iGoogle pages or some other technology, the idea of being at the mercy of the juggernaut of the Internet is unacceptable. For each of our roles as student, family member, worker, creator, thinker, we must establish various neighborhoods that help us flourish in that role. The nice thing is that we can have as few or many as we please.

---

[6] http://davidwarlick.com/wiki/pmwiki.php/Main/TheArtAmpTechniqueOfCultivating YourPersonalLearningNetwork

Will Richardson

Will Richardson, a visionary, is about the power of transformative technology and also practical as he teaches us what the real world requires of a new generation of learners. One example from his insightful blog[7] is the following advice:

A number of new Internet technologies are changing the way we find, manage and distribute information. From Weblogs, to Wikis, to RSS, to online bookmarking services, the possibilities for collaboration and sharing are almost limitless, as are the ways students and teachers can benefit in the classroom. Get an overview of the tools being used to foster this new literacy and a framework for integrating them into teaching practices.

Independent Learners

- Self-directing
- Self-selecting
- Self- editing
- Self-organizing
- Self- reflecting
- Self-publishing
- Self-connecting

"The current educational system creates and nurtures **dependent** learners. Our students depend on us to:

- create the environment in which learning takes place

- tell them what they should know, when and why

- provide the context for knowing

- provide appropriate materials for learning

- assess what they know

- select appropriate ways to share what they have learned with others

The new world of learning requires us to teach students to be **independent** learners, ones that are not dependent on teachers but are listed on the left."

Learning Commons Connections: Young people will not automatically assume the command of their own learning unless we as adults coach them to do so. Learners often feel that school is a place where adults are dictating what, how, and when to do tasks. As they begin to participate in taking command of their own learning, they become more engaged and independent. They seek more and more relevance to both now and the future.

---

[7] "An Introduction to New Internet Literacies for Educators: Blogs, Wikis, RSS, Online Bookmarking." From Will Richardson's wiki at: http://weblogged.wikispaces.com/New+Internet+Literacies

The Whole Child Initiative (ASCD)

The official statement from ASCD for their Whole Child Initiative is as follows:

Current educational practice and policy focus overwhelmingly on academic achievement. This achievement, however, is but one element of student learning and development and only a part of any complete system of educational accountability.

Together, these elements support the development of a child who is healthy, knowledgeable, motivated, and engaged. To develop the whole child requires that:

Communities provide

- Family support and involvement.
- Government, civic, and business support and resources.
- Volunteers and advocates.
- Support for their districts' coordinated school health councils or other collaborative structures.

Schools provide

- Challenging and engaging curriculum.
- Adequate professional development with collaborative planning time embedded within the school day.
- A safe, healthy, orderly, and trusting environment.
- High-quality teachers and administrators.
- A climate that supports strong relationships between adults and students.
- Support for coordinated school health councils or other collaborative structures that are active in the school.

Teachers provide

- Evidence-based assessment and instructional practices.
- Rich content and an engaging learning climate.
- Student and family connectedness.
- Effective classroom management.
- Modeling of healthy behaviors.

Learning Commons Connections: The Learning Commons is the perfect place to initiate, monitor, test, and make decisions about such initiatives as the Whole Child concerns of ASCD. Too often, such initiatives are dictated by well meaning administrators but never gain the strength needed to permeate the school. The Commons provides a checkpoint for all such shifts in program.

Professional Learning Communities

Rebecca DuFour, Richard DuFour and Robert Eaker in their plan book: *Professional Learning Communities at Work Plan Book* (Solution Tree, 2006) provides three major big ideas about professional learning communities:

Ensuring That Students Learn

A Culture of Collaboration

A Focus on Results

They see the following main shifts in doing business:
- A shift in fundamental purpose
- A shift in the use of assessments
- A shift in response when students don't learn
- A shift in the work of teachers
- A shift in focus
- A shift in school culture
- A shift in professional development

Learning Commons Connections: The Learning Commons provides a central non-threatening place in which to center the work of professional learning communities. It becomes the place for serious discussion and experimentation across the faculty so that a sense of excellence permeates the entire school. It is the place we can share, test, succeed or fail together, pick up the pieces, and move forward without stigma. This is essential if any school is to make progress as a learning community. Such communities, however, can lock out the learners. We advocate that to turn client side, representatives from the various segments of the learning community be involved, from gifted, to mainstream, to struggling.

Habits of Mind[8]

A Habit of Mind is knowing how to behave intelligently when you DON'T know the answer. A Habit of Mind means having a disposition toward behaving intelligently when confronted with problems, the answers to which are not immediately known: dichotomies, dilemmas, enigmas and uncertainties.

The 16 Habits of Mind identified by Arthur Costa and Bena Kallick include:

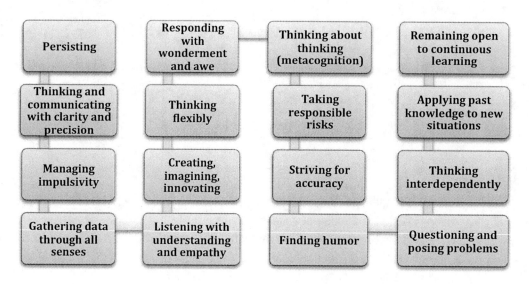

Learning Commons Connections: Habits of mind is the concept that learners should be engaged in their own learning and take control and responsibility for their own progress. The pessimist says it is not the human nature of most kids and teens. We propose that the learning experiences in both the Open Commons and the Experimental Learning Center embrace habits of mind as one of the characteristics. As we all observe in this fishbowl experience, we ask, what are the strategies that engage students and encourage self-direction and independence? It is this kind of sharing and discussion across the faculty that will enable change.

---

[8] http://www.habits-of-mind.net/

Stephen Heppell on Technology[9]

To listen to Stephen Heppell present is a real treat because of his vision and experimentation of how technology can actually change learning. On his blog, we found the following defense of technology as the enabler of learning:

Computers are everyday tools for us all, seen or unseen, but their value in learning is as tools for creativity and learning rather than as machines to develop the curriculum. These tools, in our children's hands, are forever pushing the envelope of expertise that previous technologies excluded them from: they compose and perform music before acquiring any ability to play an instrument, they shoot, edit and stream digital video before any support from media courses, they produce architectural fly-throughs of incredible buildings without any drafting or 2D skills, they make stop frame animations with their plasticine models, they edit and finesse their poetry, they explore surfaces on their visual calculators, swap ideas with scientists on-line about volcanic activity, follow webcam images of Ospreys hatching, track weather by live satellite images, control the robots they have built and generally push rapidly at the boundaries of what might be possible, indeed what was formerly possible, at any age. Little of this was easily achieved in the school classroom ten years ago although the many projects emanating from Ultralab over that decade offered clear enough indicators of what might be possible. The challenge here is to criterion referencing. So often the cry of the teacher that work is better than my degree exhibition piece, reflects a substantial step change in both the age at which a creative act can be enjoyed and the quality of the tools supporting that creativity.

Learning Commons Connections: In the early stages of technology integration in school, the learners realized quickly how to add glitz to a presentation that would appear as impressive but not necessarily substantive. Rubrics created for all products and presentations should be weighted toward excellence in content and deep understanding rather than the clever or polished use of the technology itself. Slick and polished-looking presentations need to also convey compelling messages that elevate the understanding of the audience.

---

[9] http://www.heppell.net/weblog/stephen/

International Baccalaureate Schools[10]

Mission:

The International Baccalaureate aims to develop inquiring, knowledgeable and caring young people who help to create a better and more peaceful world through intercultural understanding and respect. To this end the IB works with schools, governments and international organizations to develop challenging programs of international education and rigorous assessment. These programs encourage students across the world to become active, compassionate and lifelong learners who understand that other people, with their differences, can also be right.

KB Learners Strive to Be:

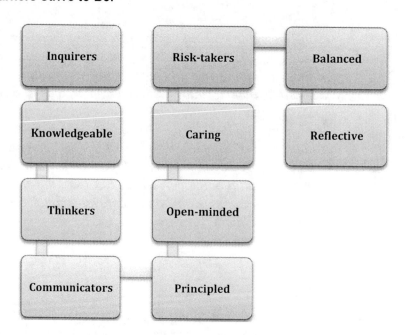

Learning Commons Connections: As we interview the creators of the IB concept, they express to us the centrality of the library as a foundational element to make their ideas work. In practice, our interviews with teacher librarians indicate that many of them are left out of the IB planning and implementation in a school. In the revised concept of the Learning Commons, this and other such global initiatives benefit from the connection to information-rich and technology-rich resources as well as the opportunities for experimentation with this great concept.

---

[10] http://www.ibo.org/

Brain Based Learning

Scientific advancements continue to unlock the mysteries of the brain. We know so much more about how the brain works, how we learn and even why some conditions for learning are better than others. To help us visualize how the brain deals with information, we have combined an Information Processing Model by Patricia Wolfe from her book *Brain Matters: Translating Research into Classroom Practice*[11] together with a model by Eric Jensen on this topic from *Teaching with the Brain in Mind.*[12]

Information Processing Model

Sensory Register
- Stimulus - sight, sound, smell, taste, touch
- Includes both conscious and nonconscious stimuli
- literally millions of bits per second

Short-Term Memory
- Usually lasts 5-20 seconds
- Only small amounts of what we take in is stored in this temporary storage buffer

Working Memory
- To retain declarative knowledge we must process it actively
- Elaboration and organization e.g. discussion, art, mapping, thinking, or debates

Long Term Memory
- Includes explicit memories that have been processed and the implicit learning
- Includes skills and conditioned responses

Learning Commons Connections: If we know how the brain learns best why aren't we doing more to design learning to take best advantage of this information? This valuable learning science can realize its potential to enhance learning in the new spaces and places of the Learning Commons. Here learning strategies and environments can be designed and trialed to create brain compatible experiences. Techniques and technology tools to help learners actively process information must be essential components of every information task to ensure that learners attain deep understanding and long lasting knowing.

---

[11] Wolfe, Patricia. *Brain Matters: Translating Research into Classroom Practice.* Alexandria, VA: Association for Curriculum Supervision and Development. 2001.

[12] Jensen, Eric. *Teaching with the Brain in Mind.* Alexandria, VA: Association for Curriculum Supervision and Development. 1998.

Differentiated Instruction

Carol Ann Tomlinson, a leader in this field, tells us that differentiation is acknowledging that kids learn in different ways, and responding by doing something about that through curriculum and instruction[13]. She explains that differentiating instruction is not an instructional strategy nor is it a teaching model. It is in fact a way of thinking, an approach, to teaching and learning that advocates beginning where students are at and designing experiences that will better help them to achieve.

In their book *Integrating Differentiated Instruction and Understanding by Design*, Tomlinson and McTighe suggest that teachers first need to establish standards for student achievement and then design many paths of instruction to enable all learners to be successful.[14] To reach desired learning standards, Tomlinson and McTighe encourage teachers to differentiate for students through the following design elements:

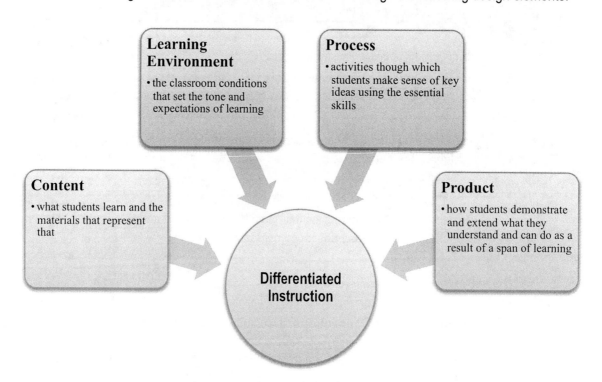

Learning Commons Connections: Driven by client-side needs and opportunities, the Learning Commons is the ultra responsive learning space. The teacher-librarian and technology specialist help classroom teachers to design differentiated learning with rich resources and technologies and strategies. Working through the Learning Commons, school leadership teams can ensure that the Tomlinson and McTighe design elements can be infused in all learning experiences.

---

[13] Tomlinson, Carol Ann. *The Differentiated Classrom*. Alexandria, VA: Association for Curriculum Supervision and Development.1999.

[14] Tomlinson, Carol Ann and McTighe Jay. *Integrating Differentiated Instruction + Understanding by Design*. Alexandria, VA: Association for Curriculum Supervision and Development.2006.

Multiple Intelligence and Five Minds for the Future

This widely accepted theory was developed by Howard Gardner, a psychologist, and professor of neuroscience from Harvard University. Over 25 years ago his classic book, *Frames of Mind: Theory of multiple intelligences* made a major impact on the education world. In that book and in later statements, he identified eight unique intelligences:

- Verbal-Linguistic Intelligence
- Musical-Rhythmic Intelligence
- Logical-Mathematical Intelligence
- Visual-Spatial Intelligence
- Bodily-Kinesthetic Intelligence
- Interpersonal Intelligence
- Intrapersonal Intelligence
- Naturalist Intelligence

Gardner's newest book, *Five Minds for the Future* outlines the specific cognitive abilities that may well illuminate future directions for 21st Century Schools.

Five Minds for the Future

The Disciplinary Mind	• The mastery of major schools of thought, including science, mathematics, and history, and of at least one professional craft.
The Synthesizing Mind	• The ability to integrate ideas from different disciplines or spheres into a coherent whole and to communicate that integration to others.
The Creating Mind	• The capacity to uncover and clarify new problems, questions and phenomena.
The Respectful Mind	• Awareness of and appreciation for differences among human beings and human groups.
The Ethical Mind	• Fulfillment of one's responsibilities as a worker and as a citizen.

Learning Commons Connections: Gardner provides grounding frameworks for the leadership teams of the Learning Commons who strive for teaching and learning environments where all learners and teachers win.

Guided Inquiry

"Guided Inquiry is carefully planned, closely supervised targeted intervention of an instructional team of school librarians and teachers to guide students through curriculum based inquiry units that build deep knowledge and deep understanding of a curriculum topic, and gradually lead towards independent learning. Guided Inquiry is grounded in a constructivist approach to learning, based on the Information Search Process developed by Kuhlthau, for developing students' competence with learning from a variety of sources while enhancing their understanding of the content areas of the curriculum."[15]

This theory has been developed by Dr. Carol C. Kuhlthau & Dr. Ross J. Todd at the Center for International Scholarship in School Libraries at Rutgers University and expanded in *Guided Inquiry: Learning in the 21st Century*. A collaborative space, designed to facilitate sharing information about the theory and practice of Guided Inquiry is found at: http://guidedinquiry.ning.com/

Six characteristics of Guided Inquiry ©

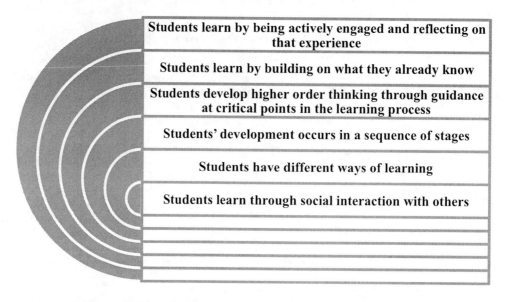

Students learn by being actively engaged and reflecting on that experience
Students learn by building on what they already know
Students develop higher order thinking through guidance at critical points in the learning process
Students' development occurs in a sequence of stages
Students have different ways of learning
Students learn through social interaction with others

Learning Commons Connections: The constructivist basis of this theory and the belief that learners share responsibility in seeking understanding, supports all work in the commons. The characteristics of Guided Inquiry are excellent criteria for measuring successful design of learning experiences in the Learning Commons.

---

[15] http://cissl.scils.rutgers.edu/guided_inquiry/introduction.html

Participatory Culture

Recent advancements in technology and the Web.02 features in particular have opened up new collaborative spaces for users. In fact Henry Jenkins and others proclaim that these advancements have spawned a unique way of creating, sharing and learning called a participatory culture.[16]

Characteristics of a Participatory Culture
- relatively low barriers to artistic expression and civic engagement
- strong support for creating and sharing one's creations with others
- some type of informal mentorship whereby what is known by the most experienced is passed along to novices
- members believe that their contributions matter
- members feel some degree of social connection with one another (at the least they care what other people think about what they have created).

The paper maintains that while not every member must contribute, all must believe they are free to contribute when ready and that what they contribute will be appropriately valued. The document also suggests that *participation* is expressed in a variety of forms; affiliations, expressions, collaborative problem solving, and circulations

Affiliations	• memberships, formal and informal, in online communities centered around various forms of media, such as Friendster, Facebook, message boards, • metagaming, game clans, or MySpace.
Expressions	• producing new creative forms, such as digital sampling, skinning and modding, fan videomaking, fan fiction writing, zines, mash-ups
Collaborative Problem-solving	• working together in teams, formal and informal, to complete tasks and develop new knowledge (such as through *Wikipedia*, alternative reality gaming, spoiling).
Circulations	• shaping the flow of media (such as podcasting, blogging).

Learning Commons Connections: The emerging participatory culture will find nourishment and inspiration in the client based organization and learning environment in the Learning Commons. Further connections to work of Henry Jenkins can be found at his blog http://www.henryjenkins.org/ and in his recent publications, *Convergence Culture* and *Fans, Bloggers and Gamers.*

---

[16] http://www.projectnml.org/files/working/NMLWhitePaper.pdf

The Current Crisis

An important Canadian report has laid bare many systemic problems for school libraries. This document, *The Crisis in Canada's School Libraries: the Case for Reform and Re-Investment*, commissioned by the Association of Canadian Publishers and Canada Heritage in 2003 has played a critical role in the battle to strengthen school library programs in Canadian schools. Designed with the policy maker in mind this valuable work provides volumes of evidence, based on research that school library programs have a positive impact on student achievement. One of the unique contributions made in this work is a formal recognition of the impact the school library has on cultural identity, socialization and citizenship. Written by Ken Haycock a champion of school libraries in Canada and everywhere, this work is a grounded starting point for change. The document can be accessed from http://www.cla.ca/slip/final_haycock_report.pdf

Dr. Haycock is professor and director of the school of Library and Information Science at San Jose State University. A recent publication *The Portable MLIS* edited by Ken Haycock and Brooke Sheldon provides a broad overview of librarianship. http://www.greenwood.com/catalog/LU5847.aspx

Learning Commons Connections: No change will happen unless all levels of educational institutions and governments recognize the need. This document goes right to the top.

Active Literacy

Active Literacy is knowing how to work information and ideas dynamically to construct meaning. Working with content curriculum today has driven the need for learners to have the ability to apply strategic thinking while reading, viewing, listening to all kinds of media, ideas and information as well as communicating their new learning. Two leaders in this movement over the years are Stephanie Harvey and Anne Goudvis. Their strategies for working with non-fiction have helped teachers understand that literacy involves working with far more than the novel. Link to their books, podcasts and recent video support at Stenhouse. http://www.stenhouse.com/html/authorbios_32.htm

Another leader in the field of active literacy is Dr. Heidi Hayes Jacobs. As well as her recent book, *Active Literacy Across the Curriculum: Strategies for Reading, Writing, Speaking and Listening*, Dr. Jacobs is president of Curriculum Designers, Inc. and offers support and professional development for schools in the areas of Interdisciplinary curriculum and curriculum mapping. http://www.curriculumdesigners.com/

Learning Commons Connections: The success of knowledge building hinges on the ability of learners to construct meaning in all disciplines. In the Learning Commons learners are not only active consumers but also active producers of information and ideas.

Administrative Leadership

Through his many publications and presentations David Booth has broadened definitions of reading and literacy to address the real world of 21st century learners. In a recent 2nd edition of the popular *Literacy Principal*, Booth now lays the groundwork for principals and school literacy leadership teams to advance schools to address the new literacies. He acknowledges the critical role teacher librarians and technology play in this process. http://www.stenhouse.com/shop/pc/viewprd.asp?idproduct=9089

David Booth is Professor Emeritus in education at the Ontario Institute for Studies in Education of the University of Toronto where he is Scholar in Residence in the Curriculum, Teaching and Language Department. Further connections to Booth's research can be found at http://www.cea-ace.ca/foo.cfm?subsection=lit&page=map&subpage=ove&subsubpage=dbo

Learning Commons Connections: The hard work involved in reinvention of school libraries and computer labs to support school wide action research and improvement requires the leadership and dedication of strong administration.

Literacy and Libraries

Connecting literacy and libraries is not always as intuitive as we would like. There are a myriad of ways to make those connections for schools. Ray Doiron and Marlene Asselin combined collective minds across Canada to explore this issue in their Publication, *Literacy, Libraries and Learning* and highlight these ideas:

- promoting reading for learning and pleasure;
- improving critical literacy skills when using information from many sources;
- encouraging research methods that respect copyright and lead to original work;
- designing information tasks to help students work effectively with data;
- developing better informational text structures that increase comprehension;
- encouraging the integration of emerging technologies and traditional resources.

Chapters of this publication can be previewed on-line at Stenhouse, http://www.stenhouse.com/shop/pc/viewprd.asp?idProduct=8972&r=&REFERER=

Learning Commons Connections: Whole school literacy is developed, initiated, and celebrated through leadership in the Learning Commons. Improving literacy achievement is an organized and coordinated effort rather than being driven by isolated projects.

Sparking the Middle Years

Adolescent learners have their own special set of needs. One of their characteristics is the need for real world relevant learning experiences. Chris Tovani coined the phrase "fake reading" in her book *I Read It but I don't Get It* and then challenges all teachers to consider reading their mandate whatever the discipline, in a later publication, *Do I Have to Teach Reading?* Information about her books and videos can be found at Chris Tovani's website *http://www.tovanigroup.com/*

Adolescents also tend to lose interest in school just at the time when they start to develop the abilities to think and reason at higher levels. In his book *Puzzle Them First: Motivating Adolescent Readers with Question Finding*, A. Vincent Ciardiello presents a powerful way to make learning relevant and engaging for learners. Published by The International Reading Association this book is a goldmine of effective strategies and a valuable approach to addressing the needs of this special group of learners.
http://www.reading.org/publications/bbv/books/bk581/abstracts/bk581-2-Ciardiello.html

Learning Commons Connections: Keeping learning real world, relevant and engaging becomes easier when the world is at the finger tips of learners and teachers. There is no "fake work" in the Learning Commons.

Effective Student Questioning

For students to fully participate and thrive in this new 'learning age', they must be critical thinkers. Questioning is the base skill that makes all thinking purposeful. **Consequently intuitive questioning techniques are becoming essential learning tools**. Through the lens of effective questions students learn to be responsible and effective information users.

Questioning skills will help every student succeed with many kinds of information tasks including:

- Exploring a topic for research
- Developing a focus for research
- Accessing information
- Validating information sources
- Designing surveys and interviews
- Processing information
- Thinking critically about information
- Deeper understanding of issues
- Connecting to real world problems and events
- Critical analysis of media texts
- Self analysis and peer review

A practical professional text to kick start staff development on effective student questioning is *Q Tasks: How to empower students to ask questions and care about answers* by Carol Koechlin and Sandi Zwaan. Selected chapters may be viewed on-line at Stenhouse.
http://www.stenhouse.com/shop/pc/viewprd.asp?idProduct=9000&r=&REFERER=

Another valuable resource to keep pace with is the Question Mark
www.questioning.org

Learning Commons Connections: Building a school wide climate conducive to inquiry is a key goal for the commons. Modeling and testing questioning strategies for all ages and disciplines is natural in this high stimulus environment.

Over to You. Discuss with Us at:http//schoollearningcommons.pbwiki.com

- What other connections to a Learning Commons concept do you recommend?

Reinventions and Transformations

and the Learning Commons

It is time to close the gap between what we know and what we do in schools. We know reading capacity improves student performance in all facets of learning. We know that technologies can be effective and efficient tools for making work easier more accurate and more fun. We know that there is a real disconnect between what our students do with technologies outside of school and what they are allowed to do with them in school. We know what the needs of 21st Century learners are and we are already behind on that schedule. We know that teacher-librarians make a significant contribution to student achievement and at the same time we see very little evidence of recognition through programs or staffing. We know that schools that employ collaborative teams for the task of school improvement make a difference, and yet isolation of specialists continues.

In the preceding chapters we have addressed this dichotomy between what we know and what we do by charting a brave shift where everyone wins. Both teachers and students will win at teaching and learning in a system that is in perpetual growth and improvement. The mantra of the Learning Commons is learning for all, for a lifetime. This final chapter provides some starting points for schools ready to reinvent their school libraries and transform teaching and learning for all.

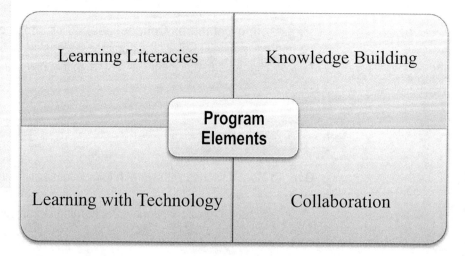

*Today's climate of reform demands that teacher-librarians become advocates for students and teachers. Being an advocate means becoming a change agent and actively and thoughtfully entering the educational conversation. It means having the language and knowledge to move beyond the library and into the wider school community. It requires familiarity with current research on teaching and learning to effectively facilitate the change process. It means carefully listening with an open mind and being responsive to teachers' concerns and questions. It means knowing how and when to communicate and whom to seek out for support. It means learning new skills to achieve the school's vision. Finally, it means being proactive and positive. Although educational change is a journey filled with uncertainty and conflict, it is an immensely rewarding one for students and adult stakeholders. **It is a journey worth leading.***

Facing the Reform Challenge: Teacher-Librarians As Change Agents By Harada, Violet H Hughes-Hassell, Sandra

So What?

Each chapter of this book ends with an *Over to You* invitation to help you explore each section a little deeper and make connections to your own school or district.

Please participate in our wiki at http//schoollearningcommons.pbwiki.com

Consciously reflect on our suggestions for the Learning Commons and keep track of new questions as well as connections to other readings and ideas you have as you work your way through each chapter. Share your ideas on the wiki. Building the Learning Commons philosophy as well as the learning spaces will take the collective minds of all.

As you make your first steps toward change consider these questions:

- What has intrigued you about the reinvention of school libraries and computer labs into a Learning Commons for all?
- What are the benefits for your school community?
- Where would the problems be?
- Where are you now?

What Next?

- ✓ Get the word out.
- ✓ Review this book with others.
- ✓ Analyze the pros and cons.
- ✓ Read the research and consider your school strengths.
- ✓ Know and understand the process of change.
- ✓ Form an inclusive planning team.
- ✓ Develop an action plan.
- ✓ Decide how you will measure success.
- ✓ Implement plans; review, reflect and reinvent as you go.
- ✓ Share the process, your problems, and your successes with others.
- ✓ Keep getting better together.

It is a Journey Worth Leading!

Glossary

Definitions in this glossary refer to the context of use in this document.

- *AASL* – The American Association of School Librarians
- *action research* –assessing and testing the impact of strategies, ideas, practices, or initiatives with actual classes of learners as they work through a new initiative. Findings apply to those particular classes, but patterns do emerge for broader use
- *active listening* – processing what is being said while it is being said vs. "in one ear and out the other"
- *administrative computing* – the computer system in the school and district that handles budgets, attendance, grades, or any other official data; well protected against hackers
- *analytical thinking* – considering information and situations from a variety of perspectives, breaking down, sorting, reorganizing, testing, making connections to empower synthesis
- *backwards planning* – application of three stages when designing a learning experience; identify desired results, determine acceptable evidence and plan learning experiences and instruction
- *big think* - an elevated group activity occurring after the creation of a product (the report, product, poster, or individual presentation) when the unit would traditionally end; all the students combine what they have learned as a group rather than end with the expertise gained by an individual investigation., to answer "So What" and "How is this new knowledge relevant ? e.g., What do we know about the significance of the African American experience; not, what do I know about the African American I studied.
- *cadres of learners* – adult or student groupings of any kind, by skill, need, interest, mixed etc.
- *calendars of the Learning Commons* – two calendars used to schedule operations of the Open Commons and the Experimental Learning Center, both open to clients on an as-need basis as opposed to former practice of scheduling classes once a week for teacher prep periods
- *client-side organization-* the needs and interests of users are paramount in planning, teaching and learning, organization, and resources, rather than putting the needs of the organization first
- *coach* - facilitate learning, create conditions conducive to learning; guide, nudge, prompt, encourage, and respond rather than tell, direct, command, etc.
- *collaboration* – planning, teaching and assessing learning experiences as a pair or group of teachers and specialists vs. teaching alone in an isolated classroom

- *collaborative knowledge building* – working together to construct understanding to build a body of knowledge
- *collaboration logs* – notes kept by classroom teachers and specialists as they co-teach a learning experience; valuable as a documentation of success and challenges, particularly useful as professional learning communities engage in serious discussion of teaching and learning
- *collection mapping* – graphical representation of the strengths and weaknesses of a collection of resources both physical and digital; a quick way to assess the current state of resources and make judgments on the direction the collection should take
- *collective intelligence* – the combined knowledge of a group where everyone has contributed
- *computer lab* – a previous model of the expanded technology services now integrated into the Learning Commons
- *co-teaching* – team teaching, two or more professionals who work together to plan, teach, coach, and assess progress of a group of learners together
- *constructivist* – a strategy of teaching that requires learners to take a great deal of the responsibility to learn the task and topic at hand
- *content instruction* – teaching of topical knowledge such as mathematics, science, social studies
- *critical thinking* – applying high level thinking and reasoning skills such as analysis, evaluation, and synthesis to develop understanding and facilitate transfer and creation
- *cross curricular* – involving more than one subject or discipline, subject integration, e.g., combining standards from social studies, music, and art in a learning experience
- *deep understanding*- making sense of the big and important ideas; relating to and able to communicate new learning
- *differentiated instruction* – learning experiences designed to ensure success for all students; modifying content, process, environment , and product to empower all learners to achieve
- *digital resources* – information and multimedia available via computer to teachers and learners at all hours of the day and night and in any location, whether at school, home, or on vacation. e.g., periodical databases, streaming video, Internet access, computer software and tools, learner-created media, ebooks, digitized textbooks, etc.
- *elastic collections* – access to, resources, rather than ownership of ; the "collection" of materials available to teachers and learners ebbs and flows as demands are placed upon it

- *empathy* – seeing and understanding another person's feelings and views about the world, understanding the reasons for differing opinions , and being able to identify with them
- *empowered learning* – learning dispositions enhanced by conditions and support, conducive to and necessary for optimum learning potential
- *engaging* – creating interest to motivate the learner to participate and achieve
- *evidence-based practice* - improving teaching and learning based on 'what works' and 'what the experts say'; gathering demonstrations of success, analyzing the evidence and then using it to change or tweak practice
- *excellence* – teaching and learning beyond minimal expectations or the specific standards
- **Experimental Learning Center** – the place both physical and virtual where professional development, action research, and experimental programs are being tests, exhibited, and analyzed before going out for widespread adoption in the rest of the school.
- *expert bar* – a service either physical or virtual, in the Learning Commons, where students and adults provide individual or small group advice and informal tutorials on software and hardware
- *extended learning* – learning in depth, for deep understanding rather than surface learning of a body of factual knowledge
- *filters* – blocks to undesirable or inappropriate Internet web sites
- **flexible scheduling** – an open calendar for the Learning Commons that invites clients (teachers or groups of learners) to reserve time to use specific physical facilities and specialists of the Learning Commons
- *formative assessments* – assessments of learning done before and during a learning experience to measure progress toward the learning goals
- *Google model* – a client-side organization where users are provided many tool choices; services they require and help create, with the philosophy that if they build it, they will use it.
- *group reflection* – looking back and assessing the impact of a learning experience done together as teachers and/or learners
- *Habits of Mind* – certain intellectual dispositions and routines systematically applied to learning situations
- *ICT literacy* – Instructional Communications Technology; the various tools of technology used to enhance the teaching and learning process

- *information coach* – one of the roles of a teacher librarian; guiding teachers and learners in how to seek, use, analyze, judge, present, and think about the vast quantities of information available
- *information literacy* – the ability to question, find quality information, consume that information with understanding, analyze and synthesize, draw conclusions, present, communication, and finally reflect on the process and the product
- *information space* – a digital space under control of the user; a personal space such as an iGoogle page or a personal website constructed by the user
- *inquiry learning* – an instructional method where students construct personal meaning by working with diverse information and ideas to solve a problem or inquiry questions; a circular process, (in which teachers are facilitators,) designed to engage students in higher levels of thinking, investigating, testing of ideas and the creation and communication of new knowledge
- *instructional computing* – the computer system in the school and district where the tools, networks, and information to support teaching and learning reside; contrary to the administrative computing, this space is open and available to all teachers and learners
- *job-embedded professional development* – is learning that occurs as educators engage in their daily work rather than transmission of knowledge and skills to teachers by experts alone; can be formal or informal, e.g., discussion, peer coaching, mentoring, study groups and action research
- *just in time* – the practice of teaching a skill at the time when that skill will be needed to pursue an assignment or project
- **knowledge building** – a constructivist activity, individual or collaborative, where inquiries and research are conducted to build deep personal understanding; understanding is advanced with planned teacher interventions such as question prompts, graphic organizers and conferencing
- *learner-constructed information systems*- client side technology systems created with input from users and designed to meet the users' need and wishes
- *Learning Commons* – the place, either physical or virtual that is the hub of the school, where exemplary teaching and learning are showcased, where all professional development, teaching and learning experimentation and action research happen; and where the various specialists of the school office, (whether virtually or physically).
- *learning dispositions* – learners' attitude and behaviors toward the learning process
- *learning experience* – any activities, taught and coached by teachers or specialists, which engage learners in the pursuit of knowledge and understanding

- *learning leadership team* – the group of adults and learner representatives working with teachers and learners to improve the quality of teaching and learning in the school
- *learning literacies leadership team* – the group of adults and learner representatives working together to create conditions to improve the skill levels of all learners and across all literacies
- *learning organization* – a school whose teachers and learners are focused on high quality teaching and learning
- *learning science*- an interdisciplinary field that studies teaching and learning to create more effective learning experiences; sciences of learning include cognitive science, educational psychology, computer science, sociology, neuroscience and other fields.
- *learning specialist* – any of the specialists in the school other than the classroom teacher, such as the teacher librarian, teacher technologist, literacy coach, etc.
- *learning to learn*- applying the many skills and behaviors associated with the process of learning itself; utilizing tools and techniques that assist in the learning process; learning how to learn as opposed to just learning content
- *library* – a predecessor of the Learning Commons
- *Library Media Center* – a predecessor of the Learning Commons
- *library web sites*- school specific sites created and maintained by staff and students to facilitate the teaching and learning needs of the school
- *literacies* – skills necessary to function successfully in school and the world at large as a "literate" citizen, lifelong learning skills including reading, writing, listening, communicating, media Literacy, visual literacy, information literacy, ICT literacy, and emerging literacies
- *literature circles* –collaborative study of student chosen reading in temporary groups; learners record their connections as they read, and at set times share. They may have roles within the study group as long as discussion is kept natural and free flowing
- *long term sustainability model*- ongoing PD, action research, rethinking and redesigning to address school needs
- *media literacy* – critical interpretation and understanding of all types of media, and creation of new media messages, e.g., seeing through the spin, being a healthy skeptic of media, advertising, messages such as political propaganda; creating a podcast to inform
- *mentor bar* – a physical and virtual service provided in the Learning Commons where strategies and advice to support teaching and learning is available to both teachers and learners

- *metacognition* – literally, thinking about one's thinking; the process of examining the strategies one uses to learn and make plans for improvement

- *Microsoft model* – a command and control organization; top down; pyramid organizational structure, with the philosophy that if we build it, they will come

- **NETS** – National Educational Technology Standards for students; a project of the International Society for Technology in Education (ISTE) that defines standards for teachers and students in the area of technology and learning

- *on demand* – just in time, instruction or coaching available when needed

- **on-demand networks** – computer networks accessible across the school campus and in the homes of teachers and learners

- **on-demand support** – available advice and troubleshooting either in person or from a distance for systems, networks, technology and services, e.g,. homework help

- *Open Commons* – The place, both physical and virtual where classes, individuals, small groups, events are scheduled to benefit from the support and expertise of specialists, the resources, and the comfortable learning environment. The Open Commons is not regularly scheduled by any group but is available using its own calendaring system. It is the place where one can observe the highest quality of teaching and learning throughout the school

- *open source* – the altruistic movement by programmers and groups of programmers to make available computer software to the masses either free or inexpensively; e.g., Open Office

- *organizational Leadership Team* - The group of professionals and learner representatives that govern the operation of the entire Learning Commons

- *peer evaluation* - assessing progress of an equal, based on predetermined criteria

- *perpetual beta* – technology, software, teaching and learning strategies, and skills continually evolving rather than being static

- *problem solving* – employing critical thinking and information literacy skills to reach a solution or understanding, e.g., finding and analyzing various perspectives on an issue to uncover causes and suggest solutions

- *professional development* – an initiative to help both teachers and specialists sharpen their skills and be more effective at their jobs

- *professional learning communities* **PLC**– groups of teachers engaged in specific discussion, experimentation, development, grant writing, and any other projects to improve teaching and learning throughout the school
- *rich learning environments* – materials, resources, and technology beyond the traditional teacher, textbook, and lecture
- *Route 21* – the initiative of the Partnership for 21st Century Learning
- *safe instructional computing systems* - *networks in which learners can flourish without interruption by unwanted guests, advertising and other bothersome messages*
- *shadow leadership*- watermark leadership, in the background; not dictating or looking over the shoulder but always there to support, guide, and assist
- *social networking* - the interaction between or linking of a group of people who share a common interest by way of discussion, sharing, and collaborating
- *specialists* – all adult professionals who consult in the Learning Commons and work with classroom teachers and learners to integrate their specialty into the curriculum of the school through both in class and pull-out programs. e.g., teacher librarians, teacher technologists, literacy coaches, nurses, counselors, art, music, history, physical education teachers; including administrators
- *summative assessments* – assessments conducted at the end of a learning experience
- *support staff* – the support staff of the Learning Commons consists of computer technicians, clericals, and assistants who handle much of the operation of the Open Commons such as circulation, processing of materials and scheduling of the Open Commons
- *sustainable excellence* – adoption of strategies across the school that are likely to continue to make a difference over time as opposed to a short-term initiative
- *teacher librarian* – the professional who is the full time information specialist in the Learning Commons and leads in the collaborative construction of learning experiences, designing collections, information literacy programs, development of the Virtual Learning Commons, development of the Virtual Exemplary Learning Center, leader in action research and professional development, Use of Web 2.0 to enhance learning,and supports for all staff and students; replacing terms librarian, library media specialist, media specialist, etc.

- *Teacher technologist* - the professional who leads the instructional computing program of the school and whose time is devoted to the integration of technology to advance teaching and learning. Often known as technology directors, teacher technologists, technology integrationists.
- *technology leadership team* – the group of adults and learner representatives who orchestrate implementation of hardware, software, and the integration of technology into teaching and learning; school leaders for instructional computing
- *Technology director* – See teacher technologist
- *technology specialist* – See the term: teacher technologist
- *tipping point* – an event that triggers a major change
- *transfer* – the ability to apply or use knowledge and understanding in new and different situations, with different topics or for different purposes
- *triangulation of evidence* – evidence collected from the organization level, the teaching unit level, and the learner level, used to compare and contrast in order to identify successes and challenges in the educational program of the school
- *user centric* – designed based on the needs, wishes, learning styles, intelligences, and *real life* habits of the users
- **Virtual Learning Commons** – consists of both an Open Commons and Experimental Learning Center, but accessible on line and available 24/7/365
- *visual literacy* – ability to read and interpret pictures, charts, illustrations; e.g., understanding how visuals can be manipulated with technology to affect the impression given
- **Web 2.0** – Tools and software available on the World Wide Web that are usually collaborative in nature and often free to anyone. E.g. wikis, blogs, nings, and a host of other creative and collaborative tools
- *wireless* – access to the Internet from anywhere in the Learning Commons on any preferred computing device without the restriction of a hard connection

Index